LEARN, TEACH...

SUCCEED...

With **REA's ILTS Test of Academic Proficiency**
test prep, you'll be in a class all your own.

WE'D LIKE TO HEAR FROM YOU!

Visit **www.rea.com** to send us your comments

ILTS

ILLINOIS LICENSURE TESTING SYSTEM

TEST OF ACADEMIC PROFICIENCY (400)

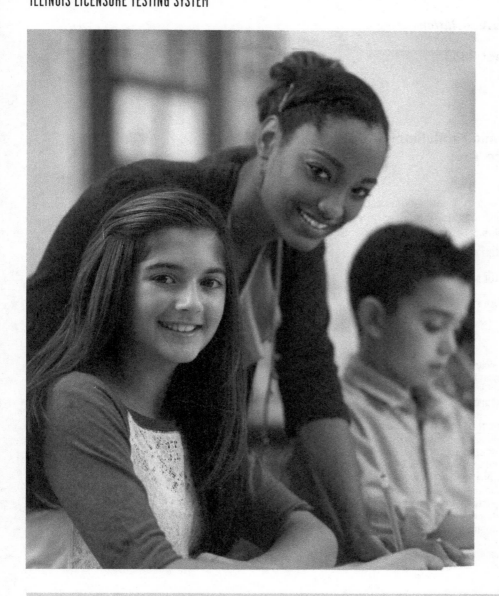

D. Antonio Cantù, Ph.D.

Patricia M. Nugent, Ph.D.

Sherrie E. Pardieck, Ed.D.

Research & Education Association

Research & Education Association
61 Ethel Road West
Piscataway, New Jersey 08854
E-mail: info@rea.com

ILTS Test of Academic Proficiency (400) with Online Practice Test

Published 2016

Printed in the United States of America

Library of Congress Control Number 2013941949

ISBN-13: 978-0-7386-1144-0
ISBN-10: 0-7386-1144-1

The ILTS Test of Academic Proficiency was developed and is administered by the Illinois State Board of Education and Pearson Education, Inc.

All trademarks cited in this publication are the property of their respective owners.

Cover image: © iStockphoto.com/CEFutcher

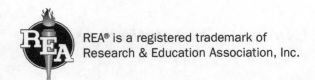

Contents

About Our Authors

Dr. D. Antonio Cantù is a Professor and Chairperson of the Department of Teacher Education at Bradley University, Peoria, Illinois. Dr. Cantù received his Ph.D. in Curriculum and Instruction from Southern Illinois University, Ed.S. in Community College Education, M.A. in History, and B.S. in Social Science Education from Arkansas State University.

Professor Cantù has over 20 years of experience in professional education from high school through the graduate level. Prior to his appointment as Chair of the Department of Teacher Education, he served as Professor and Dean of Education at Indiana University Kokomo, Professor of History and Director of Social Studies Education, as well as editor of the *International Journal of Social Education*, at Ball State University, and Social Studies Department Chair and Teacher at Ste. Genevieve (Mo.) High School.

Patricia Nugent, Ph.D., is an Associate Professor in the Department of Teacher Education at Bradley University, Peoria, Illinois. Dr. Nugent received her Ph.D. in Mathematics Education and her M.S. in Educational Administration and Foundations from Illinois State University, and her B.A. in Mathematics from Millikin University.

Sherrie Pardieck, Ed.D., is an Associate Professor in the Department of Teacher Education at Bradley University, Peoria, Illinois. Her area of specialization is the teaching of reading. Dr. Pardieck received her Ed.D. from Illinois State University, her M.A. from Bradley University, and her B.A. from Eureka College.

About REA

Founded in 1959, Research & Education Association (REA) is dedicated to publishing the finest and most effective educational materials—including study guides and test preps—for students in middle school, high school, college, graduate school, and beyond.

Today, REA's wide-ranging catalog is a leading resource for students, teachers, and other professionals. Visit *www.rea.com* to see a complete listing of all our titles.

Acknowledgments

We would like to thank Pam Weston, Publisher, for setting the quality standards for production integrity and managing the publication to completion; John Cording, Vice President, Technology, for coordinating the design and development of the REA Study Center; Larry B. Kling, Vice President, Editorial, for supervision of revisions and overall direction; Diane Goldschmidt, Managing Editor, for coordinating development of this edition; Kathy Caratozzolo of Caragraphics for typesetting this edition; Marianne L'Abbate for proofreading; Terry Casey for indexing; and Christine Saul, Senior Graphic Designer, for designing our cover.

In addition to our authors, we would like to thank the following contributors: Al Davis, M.S., M.A., David M. Myton, Ph.D., Renay M. Scott, Ph.D., Karen Bondarchuk, M.F.A., John A. Lychner, Ph.D., Janet E. Rubin, Ph.D., Ellen R. Van't Hof, M.A., Nelson Maylone, Ph.D., and Ginny Muller, Ph.D.

Introduction

Congratulations! By taking the ILTS Test of Academic Proficiency (TAP), you're on your way to a rewarding career as an Illinois teacher. Our book and the online tools that come with it give you everything you need to succeed on this important exam, bringing you one step closer to being certified to teach in the state of Illinois.

Our TAP test prep package includes:

- a complete overview of the ILTS Test of Academic Proficiency

- a comprehensive review of every standard

- an online diagnostic test to pinpoint your strengths and weaknesses and focus your study

- one full-length practice test, both in the book and online, with powerful diagnostic tools to help you personalize your prep

There are many different ways to prepare for the ILTS Test of Academic Proficiency. What's best for you depends on how much time you have to study and how comfortable you are with the subject matter. Our book has a plan that you can customize to fit both your lifestyle and study style.

HOW TO USE THIS BOOK

About the Review

The review chapters in this book are designed to help you sharpen the basic skills needed to pass the ILTS Test of Academic Proficiency. The exam is composed of four subtests that assess your knowledge of fundamental skills in the following areas: Reading Comprehension, Language Arts, Mathematics, and Writing. Each of the skills required for all four subtests is discussed at length to optimize your understanding of what the Test of Academic Proficiency covers.

Keep in mind that your schooling has taught you most of what you need to know to answer the questions on the test. Our review is designed to help you fit the information you have acquired into specific competency components. Studying your class notes and textbooks together with our reviews will give you an excellent foundation for passing the exam.

About the REA Study Center

The best way to personalize your study plan is to get feedback on what you know and what you don't know. At the online REA Study Center, we give you a diagnostic practice test plus one full-length practice test with detailed score reports that pinpoint your strengths and weaknesses.

Before you review with the book, go to the REA Study Center and take the Diagnostic Test. Armed with your score report, you can personalize your study plan. Review the parts of the book where you're weakest and focus your study on the areas where you need the most review.

After reviewing with the book, take the Practice Test online at the REA Study Center to ensure that you have mastered the material and are ready for test day. Use your score reports to identify any other areas where you need extra study, and read those sections of the review chapters again.

If you are studying and don't have Internet access, you can take the printed tests in the book. These are the same practice tests offered at the REA Study Center, but without the added benefits of timed testing conditions, automatic scoring, and diagnostic score reports.

AN OVERVIEW OF THE TEST

What is the Purpose of the ILTS Test of Academic Proficiency?

While passing the ILTS Test of Academic Proficiency alone is not sufficient to earn a license to teach in Illinois, it is required, in addition to the completion of courses of study, and successfully passing the appropriate content-area test(s) and Assessment of Professional Teaching (APT).

Along with other required content-area tests, the Test of Academic Proficiency is required if you:

- want to get the **Early Childhood**, **Elementary**, **Secondary**, or **Special Teaching** License;

- want to get a **School Service Personnel or Administrative license**;

- are a teacher in an **alternative route program**;

- are an out-of-state candidate applying for a Professional Educator License; and/or

- seek admission into an **Illinois-approved educator preparation program** (you must successfully complete the Test of Academic Proficiency before being admitted to the program).

The Test of Academic Proficiency Standards are included in the appendix. In addition, more information about who needs to take the TAP is available at the Illinois State Board of Education's Educator Licensure website (*www.isbe.net/certification/*).

Further information about the ILTS Test of Academic Proficiency is also available in the Illinois Licensure Testing System Registration Bulletin, which can be found online at *www.il.nesinc.com*.

What is Tested on the ILTS Test of Academic Proficiency?

The Illinois Licensure Testing System tests are aligned with the Illinois professional teaching standards and content-area standards for educators. The ILTS tests are the only tests accepted for licensure in Illinois.

The Test of Academic Proficiency consists of 170 multiple-choice questions in Reading Comprehension, Language Arts, and Mathematics, as well as one written constructed-response writing assignment, distributed as follows:

Subtest	Number of Questions
I. Reading Comprehension	60
II. Language Arts	60
III. Mathematics	50
IV. Writing	1 written response

Common Core State Standards and the Test of Academic Proficiency

Although the Illinois State Board of Education (ISBE) did not produce any specific alignment table or document relative to Common Core State Standards and TAP test alignment, the current TAP test is reflective of ISBE's attempt to ensure its alignment with the Common Core State Standards.

The mathematics section of the TAP now includes questions on probability. Specifically, the test includes two questions in which the candidate must demonstrate knowledge of basic concepts of probability, using a variety of representations (e.g., word problems, Venn diagrams, tree diagrams).

What is the format of the ILTS Test of Academic Proficiency?

During this computer-based test, you must select your answers to multiple-choice questions on the computer screen and type your response to the writing assignment. If you are taking all four subtests, you will have a total of five hours to complete the entire test. You should allow approximately 60 minutes to complete your written response, thus devoting the remaining 4 hours to the multiple-choice questions. If you are taking one-subtest, you will have a total of two hours and thirty minutes to complete the subtest.

You should have plenty of time to complete the test, but be aware of the amount of time you are spending on each question so you allow yourself time to complete the whole test. Try to maintain a steady pace when answering questions. Using our online practice tests with timed testing conditions will help you use your time efficiently.

Passing subtest scores will be banked. As a result, individuals will only need to complete subtests they have not yet passed. You can take the subtests as necessary until you pass.

How Do I Register for the Test and Is There a Registration Fee?

Individuals may register for the computer-based Test of Academic Proficiency online by clicking on the "Register Now" link on the ILTS website. Be sure to register far in advance of the desired test date, given seating is limited and appointments are scheduled on a first-come, first-served basis. If you take all four subtests of the TAP in a single sitting, the total fee is $125. If you choose to take a single subtest, the total fee is $75.

When and Where Can I Take the Exam?

The Test of Academic Proficiency is available only as a computer-based test. Refer to "Test Sites for Computer-Based Testing" at *www.il.nesinc.com/* for information about available test centers. Computer-based testing (CBT) is made available year-round, by appointment only, Monday through Saturday (with the exception of holidays) at 225 test centers throughout the United States and its territories.

The ILTS Test of Academic Proficiency is developed by the state of Illinois and administered by the Illinois Licensure Testing System/Pearson Education, Inc. Additional information on the Test of Academic Proficiency is available from the Illinois State Board of Education (ISBE), to which Pearson Education is under contract. Contact information for ISBE, ILTS/Pearson are listed below:

Illinois State Board of Education
100 N. 1st Street
Springfield, IL 62777
Phone: (866) 262-6663
Website: *www.isbe.net/certification*

Illinois Licensure Testing System
Evaluation Systems
Pearson
P.O. Box 660
Amherst, MA 01004-9000
Website: *www.il.nesinc.com*

SCORING THE ILTS TEST OF ACADEMIC PROFICIENCY

The Illinois Licensure Testing System reports the Test of Academic Proficiency official score to all test-takers, the Illinois State Board of Education, and to any institution the test-taker identifies during registration. Each subtest score is reported on a scale of 100 to 300, with a minimum scaled test score of 240 required to pass each of the respective subtests. A subtest score is based on the number of multiple-choice questions answered correctly; as a result, test-takers do not lose any points for wrong answers. The multiple-choice portion of the test is scored by computer.

For the writing portion of the TAP, at least two evaluators review the essay, and it is scored not on the opinions expressed, but rather on focus (clear main idea), support/elaboration (with examples and details), organization, and grammar/conventions. Because a six-point scale is used (six being the highest), each evaluator gives a score and then the two scores are added together. If the scores differ by more than two points, a third reader is brought in. Ultimately, the score (out of 12) is converted to a 100- to 300-point score (again with 240 or above being a pass). In a worst-case scenario, an evaluator would issue a score of "U" (which means "unscorable") for responses that are illegible, off-topic, indecipherable due to second language issues, or too short.

REA's online diagnostic test and practice test are scored automatically to give you an idea of how you'll do on test day. If you do not get a passing score on the diagnostic test or the practice tests, review your online score report and study the detailed explanations for the questions you answered incorrectly. Note which types of questions you answered wrong, and re-examine the corresponding review. After further review, you may want to re-take the practice tests online.

When Will I Receive My Score Report?

Individuals may access their Test of Academic Proficiency score report online at 10:00 p.m. Central Time on the score report date that is listed at the "Score Reporting" link on the ILTS website. TAP score reports are made available for a period of 45 days, as a PDF file, which may be printed and saved. Official TAP test scores are reported within two to four weeks after the test date. In addition, many of the Pearson Test Centers make available *unofficial* TAP test results for the multiple-choice subtests immediately following testing.

Every score report contains a section titled "How to Read Your Score Report," which helps to interpret the results. Additional information on the score report is also available on the ILTS website link, "Release of Your Test Scores."

Can I Retake the Test?

If you do not do well on test day, don't panic! Subtests can be retaken, so you can work on improving your score on your next try. A score on the Test of Academic Proficiency that does not match your expectations does not mean you should change your plans about entering the teaching profession.

Once registered for an ILTS computer-based test, individuals must wait until after the test is completed to register for the same computer-based test again. In addition, individuals must wait 60 days after taking the computer-based Test of Academic Proficiency before retaking it.

STUDYING FOR THE ILTS TEST OF ACADEMIC PROFICIENCY

How Do I Begin Studying?

There is no one correct way to study for the ILTS Test of Academic Proficiency. Some test-takers prefer to set aside a few hours every morning to study, while others prefer to study at night before going to sleep. Only you can determine when and where your study time will be most effective. Here are a few suggestions to get you started.

1. To best utilize your study time, follow our ILTS TAP Study Schedule on page 9. The schedule is based on a six-week study program, but it can be condensed to three weeks if necessary.

2. Take the diagnostic test online at *www.rea.com/studycenter.*

3. Study the review chapters.

4. Spend time reviewing topics that give you the most trouble.

5. Take our online practice test and review your diagnostic score report. Study the review material where you need to improve. Read the detailed answer explanations for questions you answered wrong.

When Should I Start Studying?

Scheduling your study time wisely is a key component to your success on the ILTS Test of Academic Proficiency.

Remember, it is never too early to start studying for the Test of Academic Proficiency. The earlier you begin, the more time you will have to sharpen your skills and focus your efforts. Do not procrastinate. Cramming is not an effective way to study, since it does not allow you enough time to learn the test material. Make the most of your study time while you have it. Use it well to master the essentials necessary to pass. Work out a study routine and stick to it. Reviewing class notes and textbooks along with our book will provide you with an even better foundation for passing the Test of Academic Proficiency.

When you take the diagnostic test and practice test, simulate the conditions of the actual test as closely as possible. Turn your television and radio off, and sit down at a quiet table free from distraction.

As you complete each test, review your score reports, study the diagnostic feedback, and thoroughly review the explanations to the questions you answered incorrectly. However, do not review too much at any one time. Concentrate on one problem area at a time by reviewing the question and explanation, and by studying our review until you are confident that you have mastered the material. Give extra attention to the reviews that cover your areas of difficulty, as this will build your skills in those areas.

STUDY SCHEDULE

Although our study plan is designed to be used in the six weeks before the exam, it can be condensed or expanded to suit your schedule. Be sure to set aside enough time (at least two hours each day) to study. The more time you spend studying, the more prepared and confident you will be on the day of the test.

Week	Activity
1	**Take the online diagnostic exam at the REA Study Center.** Your detailed score report will identify topics where you need the most review. Afterward, review the explanations for questions you answered incorrectly.
2	**Study the review chapters.** Use your score report from the diagnostic test to focus your study. Useful study techniques include highlighting key terms and information and taking notes as you read the review, noting new terms and facts.
3	**Reread all your notes, refresh your understanding of the exam's competencies, review your college textbooks, and read class notes you've taken.** This is also the time to consider any other supplementary materials that your advisor suggests.
4	**Take the online practice test at the REA Study Center.** The detailed score report will identify topics where you need further review.
5	**Condense your notes.** A structured list of important facts and concepts, based on your notes and the book's competencies, will help you thoroughly review for the test. Review the answers and explanations for all missed questions on the Diagnostic Test and Practice Test.
6	**Retake the diagnostic test at the REA Study Center to see how much your score has improved.** If you still got a few questions wrong, go back to the review and study any topics you missed.

TEST-TAKING TIPS

Taking an important standardized test like the ILTS might make you nervous. These test tips will help alleviate your test-taking anxieties.

Tip 1. Become comfortable with the format of the test. When you are practicing, stay calm and pace yourself. After simulating the test only once, you will boost your chances of doing well, and you will be able to sit down for the actual ILTS TAP with much more confidence.

Tip 2. Familiarize yourself with the directions on the test. This will not only save time but will also help you avoid anxiety (and the mistakes anxiety causes).

Tip 3. Read all of the possible answers. Just because you think you have found the correct response, do not automatically assume that it is the best answer. Read through each choice to be sure that you are not making a mistake by jumping to conclusions.

Tip 4. Use the process of elimination. Go through each answer choice and eliminate as many as possible. If you can eliminate one or two answer choices, you will give yourself a better chance of getting the item correct since there will be fewer choices left from which to make your guess. Do not leave an answer blank; it is better to guess than to not answer a question as there is no penalty for incorrect answers.

Tip 5. Work at a steady pace and avoid focusing on any one question too long. Taking the timed practice tests online at the REA Study Center will help you learn to budget your time.

Tip 6. When taking the computer-based exam, be sure your answer registers before you go to the next item. Look at the screen to see that your mouse click causes the pointer to darken the proper oval. If your answer doesn't register, you won't get credit for that question.

The Day of the Test

Check your registration information to find out what time to arrive at the testing center. Make sure you arrive early. This will allow you to collect your thoughts and relax before the test, and will also spare you the anguish that comes with being late. (If you arrive late, you might not be admitted to the test center.)

Check your admission ticket 24 hours before the test in case there is a change. If there is a change, you will have to print out a new ticket.

Before you leave for the test center, make sure that you have your admission ticket and two forms of identification, one of which must contain a recent and recognizable photograph, your name, and signature (i.e., driver's license). All documents must be originals (no copies). You will not be admitted to the test center and you will forfeit your test fees if you do not have proper identification. (More information about proper forms of ID is listed in the official registration booklet.)

Be prepared to have your photograph taken at the test center. Your photo will appear with your unofficial test results at the end of the test session.

Dress comfortably so you are not distracted by being too hot or too cold while taking the test.

You may wear a watch to the test center. However, you may not wear one that makes noise, because it may disturb the other test-takers.

Do not bring cell phones, smartphones and other electronic, listening, recording, or photographic devices into the test center. Dictionaries, textbooks, notebooks, calculators, briefcases, or packages are also not permitted. If you bring these devices into the test center, you will be dismissed from the test, your fee will be forfeited, and your test scores will be canceled.

Procedures will be followed to maintain test security. Once you enter the test center, follow all of the rules and instructions given by the test supervisor. If you do not, you risk being dismissed from the test and having your scores cancelled.

After the Test

When you finish your test go home and relax—you deserve it!

Good luck on the ILTS Test of Academic Proficiency!

Reading Comprehension

The reading portion of the Test of Academic Proficiency asks the test-taker to utilize critical reading and reading comprehension skills. The objectives for this section of the test are to understand the main ideas of the passage based on the supporting evidence or details and to understand the author's purpose, point of view, and/or intended meaning.

Test-takers will be asked to read a passage and answer questions about the material included in that passage. The reading section is entirely multiple choice. It will be to your benefit to read the questions about the particular passage first. This will give you an idea of what to look for and focus on as you are reading. It is also crucial that you understand the passage as a whole and comprehend the overall intention, meaning, or main idea of the material you have read.

This chapter was written to prepare you for the reading section of the Test of Academic Proficiency. You will be guided through a step-by-step approach to attacking reading passages and questions. Also included are tips to help you quickly and accurately answer the questions that will appear in this section. By studying this review and taking the practice test, you will be more aware of the broad range of objectives that are covered in the Test of Academic Proficiency Standards 1, 2, 3, 4, 5, and 6.

Remember, the more you know about the skills tested, the better you will perform on the test. In this section, the objectives you will be tested on are contained in the following list:

Fast Facts

The more you know about the skills tested, the better you will perform on the test.

Standard 1   **Determine the meaning of words and phrases in context.**

The following are examples of content that may be covered under this standard.

1.1   Use context clues to determine the meaning of unfamiliar words or words with multiple meanings.

1.2   Recognize the correct use of commonly misused pairs (e.g., affect/effect) in a passage.

1.3   Determine the meaning of figurative or colloquial language in a passage.

1.4   Identify appropriate synonyms or antonyms for words in a passage.

Standard 2   **Understand the main idea and supporting details in written material.**

The following are examples of content that may be covered under this standard.

2.1   Identify the stated main idea of a paragraph or passage.

2.2   Establish the sequence of events or steps presented in a passage.

2.3   Recognize information that supports, illustrates, or elaborates the main idea of a paragraph or a passage.

2.4   Identify the meaning of a figurative expression in a passage.

Standard 3   **Apply skills of inference and interpretation to a variety of written materials.**

The following are examples of content that may be covered under this standard.

3.1   Recognize a writer's implied purpose for writing (e.g., to persuade, to describe).

3.2   Identify the statement that best expresses the implied main idea of a paragraph or passage.

3.3   Recognize implied cause-and-effect relationships in a passage.

3.4   Interpret the content, word choice, and phrasing of a passage to determine a writer's opinions, point of view, or position on an issue.

Standard 4   **Analyze relationships among ideas in written material.**

The following are examples of content that may be covered under this standard.

4.1   Recognize similarities and differences among ideas in a passage.

4.2   Analyze relationships between ideas in opposition (e.g., pro and con).

4.3   Select solutions to problems based on information presented in written material.

4.4   Draw conclusions from information stated or implied in a passage.

Standard 5   **Use critical reasoning skills to evaluate written material.**

The following are examples of content that may be covered under this standard.

5.1   Recognize stated or implied assumptions on which the validity of an argument depends.

5.2   Determine the relevance of specific facts, examples, or graphic data to a writer's argument.

5.3   Recognize fallacies in the logic of a writer's argument.

5.4   Recognize qualifying language and distinguish between fact and opinion in written material.

5.5   Assess the credibility, objectivity, or bias of the author of a passage or the author's sources.

Standard 6   **Apply skills for outlining and summarizing written materials and interpreting information presented in graphs or tables.**

The following are examples of content that may be covered under this standard.

6.1   Organize the main ideas in a passage into an outline or another form of graphic or tabular organization.

6.2   Identify an accurate summary of a passage.

6.3   Interpret information presented in charts, graphs, or tables.

To help you master these skills, we present examples of the types of questions you will encounter and explanations of how to answer them.

THE PASSAGES

The reading passages in the reading section are designed to be on the level of the type of material encountered in college textbooks. They will present you with very diverse subjects. Although you will not be expected to have prior knowledge of the information presented in the passages, you will be expected to know the fundamental reading comprehension techniques presented in this chapter. Only your ability to read and comprehend material will be tested.

THE QUESTIONS

Each passage will be followed by a number of questions. The questions will ask you to make determinations based on what you have read. You will commonly encounter questions that will ask you to:

- Determine which of the given answer choices best expresses the main idea of the passage.

- Determine the author's purpose in writing the passage.

- Determine which fact best supports the writer's main idea.

- Know the difference between fact and opinion in a statement.

- Organize the information in the passage.

- Determine which of the answer choices best summarizes the information presented in the passage.

- Recall information from the passage.

- Analyze cause-and-effect relationships based on information in the passage.

- Determine the definition and identify the meaning of a word as it is used in the passage.

- Answer a question based on information presented in graphic form.

- Determine the correct use of commonly misused word pairs such as *their*, *there* and *they're*.

STRATEGIES FOR THE READING SECTION

The following is a recommended plan of attack for answering the questions in the reading section.

When reading the passage,

Step 1: Read quickly while keeping in mind that questions will follow.

Step 2: Uncover the main idea or theme of the passage. Many times it is contained within the first few lines of the passage.

Step 3: Uncover the main idea of each paragraph. Usually it is contained in either the first or last sentence of the paragraph.

Step 4: Skim over the detailed points of the passage while circling key words or phrases. These are words or phrases such as *but*, *on the other hand*, *although*, *however*, *yet*, and *except*. These words are conjunctions or phrases that connect thoughts and can provide additional conditions on the statements.

When answering the questions,

Step 1: Approach each question one at a time. Read it carefully.

Step 2: Uncover the main idea or theme of the passage. Many times it is contained within the first few lines of the passage.

Step 3: If the question is asking for an answer that can be found only in a specific place in the passage, save it for last since this type of question requires you to go back to the passage and therefore takes more of your time.

Additional Tips

- Read over the questions before reading the passage. This will give you an idea of what you are reading for.

- Look over all the passages first and then attack the passages that seem easiest and most interesting.

- Identify and underline what sentences are the main ideas of each paragraph.

- If a question asks you to draw inferences, your answer should reflect what is implied in the passage, rather than what is directly stated.

- Use the context of the sentence to find the meaning of an unfamiliar word.

- Identify what sentences are example sentences and label them with an "E." Determine whether or not the writer is using facts or opinions.

- Circle key transitions and identify dominant patterns of organization.

- Make your final response and move on. Don't dawdle or get frustrated by the really troublesome passages. If you haven't gotten answers after two attempts, answer as best you can and move on.

- If you have time at the end, go back to the passages that were difficult and review them again.

A FOUR-STEP APPROACH

When you take the reading section of the test, you will have two tasks: to read the passage and to answer the questions.

Of the two, carefully reading the passage is the more important; answering the questions is based on an understanding of the passage. What follows is a four-step approach to reading:

> **Step 1:** Preview.
>
> **Step 2:** Read actively.
>
> **Step 3:** Review the passage.
>
> **Step 4:** Answer the questions.

You should study the following exercises and use these four steps when you complete the reading section of the TAP.

STEP 1: PREVIEW

A preview of the reading passage will give you a purpose and a reason for reading; previewing is a good strategy to use when taking a test. Before beginning to read the passage (usually a four-minute activity if you preview and review), you should take about thirty seconds to look over the passage and questions. An effective way to preview the passage is to quickly read the first sentence of each paragraph, the concluding sentence of the passage, and the questions—but not the answers—following the passage.

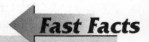

Fast Facts

A preview of the reading passage will give you a purpose and a reason for reading.

Below is a passage about the Supreme Court's handling of obscenity and pornography. Practice previewing the following passage by reading the first sentence of each paragraph, the last line of the passage, and the 11 questions that follow the passage. Throughout the remainder of this chapter we will analyze the questions and discuss the correct and incorrect answers.

Passage

That the area of obscenity and pornography is a difficult one for the Supreme Court is well documented. The Court's numerous attempts to define obscenity have proven unworkable and left the decision to the subjective preferences of the justices. Perhaps Justice Stewart put it best when, after refusing to define obscenity, he declared, but "I know it when I see it." Does the Court literally have to see it to know it? Specifically, what role does the fact-pattern, including the materials' medium, play in the Court's decision?

Several recent studies employ fact-pattern analysis in modeling the Court's decision making. These studies examine the fact-pattern or case characteristics, often with ideological and attitudinal factors, as a determinant of the decision reached by the Court. In broad terms, these studies owe their theoretical underpinnings to attitude theory. As the name suggests, attitude theory views the Court's attitudes as an explanation of its decisions.

These attitudes, however, do not operate in a vacuum. As Spaeth explains, "[t]he activation of an attitude involves both an object and the situation in which that object is encountered." The objects to which the Court directs its attitudes are litigants. The situation—the subject matter of the case—can be defined in broad or narrow terms. One may define the situation as an entire area of the law (e.g., civil liberties issues). On an even broader scale, the situation may be defined as the decision to grant certiorari or whether to defect from a minimum-winning coalition.

Defining the situation with such broad strokes, however, does not allow one to control for case content. In many specific issue areas, the cases present strikingly similar patterns. In examining the Court's search and seizure decisions, Segal found that a relatively small number of situational and case characteristic variables explain a high proportion of the Court's decisions.

Despite Segal's success, efforts to verify the applicability of fact-pattern analysis in other issue areas and using broad-based factors have been slow in forthcoming. Renewed interest in obscenity and pornography by federal and state governments as a result of lobbying campaigns by fundamentalist groups, the academic community, and other antipornography interest groups pro and con indicate the Court's decisions in this area deserve closer examination.

The Court's obscenity and pornography decisions also present an opportunity to study the Court's behavior in an area where the Court has granted significant decision-making authority to the states. In *Miller v. California* (1973) the Court announced the importance of local community standards in obscenity determinations. The Court's subsequent behavior may suggest how the Court will react in other areas where it has chosen to defer to the states (e.g., abortion).

Questions

1. The main idea of the passage is best stated in which of the following?

    A. The Supreme Court has difficulty convicting those who violate obscenity laws.

    B. The current definitions for obscenity and pornography provided by the Supreme Court are unworkable.

    C. Fact-pattern analysis is insufficient for determining the attitude of the Court toward the issues of obscenity and pornography.

    D. Despite the difficulties presented by fact-pattern analysis, Justice Segal found the solution in the patterns of search and seizure decisions.

2. The main purpose of the writer in this passage is to

    A. convince the reader that the Supreme Court is making decisions about obscenity based on their subjective views alone.

    B. explain to the reader how fact-pattern analysis works with respect to cases of obscenity and pornography.

    C. define obscenity and pornography for the layperson.

    D. demonstrate the role fact-pattern analysis plays in determining the Supreme Court's attitude about cases in obscenity and pornography.

3. Of the following, which fact best supports the writer's contention that the Court's decisions in the areas of obscenity and pornography deserve closer scrutiny?

    A. The fact that a Supreme Court Justice said, "I know it when I see it."

B. Recent studies that employ fact-pattern analysis in modeling the Court's decision-making process.

C. The fact that attitudes do not operate in a vacuum.

D. The fact that federal and state governments, interested groups, and the academic community have shown renewed interest in the obscenity and pornography decisions by the Supreme Court.

4. Among the following statements, which states an opinion expressed by the writer rather than a fact?

A. It is well documented that the area of obscenity and pornography is a difficult one for the Supreme Court.

B. The objects to which a court directs its attitudes are the litigants.

C. In many specific issue areas, the cases present strikingly similar fact-patterns.

D. The Court's subsequent behavior may suggest how the Court will react in other legal areas.

5. The group of topics in the list that follows that best reflects the organization of the topics of the passage is

A.   I.   The difficulties of the Supreme Court
      II. Several recent studies
      III. Spaeth's definition of *attitude*
      IV. The similar patterns of cases
      V. Other issue areas
      VI. The case of *Miller v. California*

B.   I.   The Supreme Court, obscenity, and fact-pattern analysis
      II. Fact-pattern analyses and attitude theory
      III. The definition of *attitude* for the Court
      IV. The definition of *situation*
      V. The breakdown in fact-pattern analysis
      VI. Studying Court behavior

C. I.   Justice Stewart's view of pornography
II. Theoretical underpinnings
III. A minimum-winning coalition
IV. Search and seizure decisions
V.   Renewed interest in obscenity and pornography
VI. The importance of local community standards

D. I.   The Court's numerous attempts to define obscenity
II. Case characteristics
III. The subject matter of cases
IV. The Court's proportion of decisions
V.   Broad-based factors
VI. Obscenity determination

6. Which paragraph among those that follow is the best summary of the passage?

A. The Supreme Court's decision-making process with respect to obscenity and pornography has become too subjective. Fact-pattern analyses used to determine the overall attitude of the Court reveal only broad-based attitudes on the part of the Court toward the situations of obscenity cases. But these patterns cannot fully account for the Court's attitudes toward case content. Research is not conclusive on whether fact-pattern analyses work when applied to legal areas. Renewed public and local interest suggests continued study and close examination of how the Court makes decisions. Delegating authority to the states may reflect patterns for Court decisions in other socially sensitive areas.

B. Though subjective, the Supreme Court decisions are well documented. Fact-pattern analyses reveal the attitude of the Supreme Court toward its decisions in cases. Spaeth explains that an attitude involves both an object and a situation. For the Court, the situation may be defined as the decision to grant certiorari. Cases present strikingly similar patterns, and a small number of variables explain a high proportion of the Court's decisions. Segal has made an effort to verify the applicability of fact-pattern analysis with some success. The Court's decisions on obscenity and pornography suggest weak Court behavior, such as in *Miller v. California*.

C. To determine what obscenity and pornography mean to the Supreme Court, we must use fact-pattern analysis. Fact-pattern analysis reveals the ideas that the Court uses to operate in a vacuum. The litigants and the subject matter of cases are defined in broad terms (such as an entire area of law) to reveal the Court's decision-making process. Search and seizure cases reveal strikingly similar patterns, leaving the Court open to grant certiorari effectively. Renewed public interest in the Court's decisions proves how the Court will react in the future.

D. Supreme Court decisions about pornography and obscenity are under examination and are out of control. The Court has to see the case to know it. Fact-pattern analyses reveal that the Court can only define cases in narrow terms, thus revealing individual egotism on the part of the Justices. As a result of strikingly similar patterns in search and seizure cases, the Court should be studied further for its weakness in delegating authority to state courts, as in the case of *Miller v. California*.

7. Based on the passage, the rationale for fact-pattern analyses arises out of what theoretical groundwork?

A. Subjectivity theory

B. The study of cultural norms

C. Attitude theory

D. Cybernetics

8. Based on data in the passage, what would most likely be the major cause for the difficulty in pinning down the Supreme Court's attitude toward cases of obscenity and pornography?

A. The personal opinions of the Court Justices

B. The broad nature of the situations of the cases

C. The ineffective logistics of certiorari

D. The inability of the Court to resolve the variables presented by individual case content

9.   In the context of the passage, *subjective* might be most nearly defined as

   A.   personal.

   B.   wrong.

   C.   focused.

   D.   objective.

10.   What would be a possible solution for the Supreme Court's obscenity and pornography decision-making process?

   A.   Administer a fact-pattern analysis to gather data on every obscenity and pornography case.

   B.   Define the legal terms of obscenity and pornography.

   C.   Continue to look at each obscenity and pornography case individually taking into account the Court's subjectivity.

   D.   Control case content with broad definitions of obscenity and pornography.

11.   Which of the following offers a valid conclusion a reader may reach after reading the passage?

   A.   The Supreme Court functions in a vacuum.

   B.   Popular case content affects patterns in court decisions.

   C.   The Supreme Court intends to define the terms of obscenity and pornography.

   D.   A change in the makeup of the Supreme Court Justices could affect the decisions made on obscenity and pornography cases.

By previewing the passage, you should have read the following:

   •   It is well documented that the areas of obscenity and pornography are difficult ones for the Supreme Court.

   •   Several recent studies employ fact-pattern analysis in modeling the Court's decision making.

- These attitudes, however, do not operate in a vacuum.

- Defining the situation with such broad strokes, however, does not allow one to control for case content.

- Despite Segal's success, efforts to verify the applicability of fact-pattern analysis in other issue areas and using broad-based factors have been slow in coming.

- The Court's obscenity and pornography decisions also present an opportunity to study the Court's behavior in an area where the Court has granted significant decision-making authority to the states.

- The Court's subsequent behavior may suggest how the Court will react in other areas where it has chosen to defer to the states (e.g., abortion).

These few sentences tell you much about the entire passage. As you begin to examine the passage, you should first determine the main idea of the passage and underline it so you can easily refer to it if a question requires (see question 1). The main idea should be found in the first paragraph of the passage, and may even be the first sentence. From what you have read thus far, you now know that the main idea of this passage is that the Supreme Court has difficulty in making static decisions about obscenity and pornography.

In addition, you also know that recent studies have used fact-pattern analysis in modeling the Court's decisions. You have learned that attitudes do not operate independently and that case content is important. The feasibility of using fact-pattern analysis in other areas and broad-based factors have not been quickly verified. To study the behavior of the Court in an area in which it has granted significant decision-making authority to the states, one has only to consider the obscenity and pornography decisions. In summary, the author suggests that the Court's subsequent behavior may suggest how the Court will react in those other areas in which decision-making authority has previously been ceded to the states. As you can see, having this information will make the reading of the passage much easier.

You should have also looked at the stem of the question in your preview. You do not necessarily need to spend time reading the answers to each question in your preview. The stem alone can help to guide you as you read.

The stems in this case are:

1. The main idea of the passage is best stated in which of the following?

2. The main purpose of the writer in this passage is to _____?

3. Of the following, which fact best supports the writer's contention that the Court's decisions in the areas of obscenity and pornography deserve closer scrutiny?

4. Among the following statements, which states an opinion expressed by the writer rather than a fact?

5. The group of topics in the list that follows that best reflects the organization of the topics of the passage is _____.

6. Which paragraph among those that follow is the best summary of the passage?

7. Based on the passage, the rationale for fact-pattern analyses arises out of what theoretical groundwork?

8. Based on data in the passage, what would most likely be the major cause for the difficulty in pinning down the Supreme Court's attitude toward cases of obscenity and pornography?

9. In the context of the passage, *subjective* might be most nearly defined as _____.

10. What would be a possible solution for the Supreme Court's obscenity and pornography decision-making process?

11. Which of the following offers a valid conclusion a reader may reach after reading the passage?

STEP 2: READ ACTIVELY

After your preview, you are now ready to read actively. This means that, as you read, you will be engaged in such things as underlining important words, topic sentences, main ideas, and words denoting the tone of a passage. If you think underlining can help you save time and help you remember the main ideas, feel free to use your pencil.

Read the first sentence of each paragraph carefully, because this often contains the topic of the paragraph. You may wish to underline each topic sentence.

During this stage, you should also determine the writer's purpose in writing the passage, as this will help you focus on the main points and the writer's key points in the organization of a passage.

You can determine the author's primary goal or overall objective by asking yourself whether the relationship between the writer's main idea and the evidence the writer uses can answer one of the following questions:

- Is the writer trying to persuade you by proving or using facts to make a case for an idea?

- Is the writer trying only to inform and enlighten you about an idea, object, or event?

- Is the writer attempting to amuse you? To keep you fascinated or laughing?

Read the paragraphs about jogging below and decide what the primary purpose of each statement is.

(1) Jogging too late in life can cause more health problems than it solves. I will allow that the benefits of jogging are many: lowered blood pressure, increased vitality, better cardiovascular health, and better muscle tone. However, an older person may have a history of injury or chronic ailments that makes jogging counterproductive. For example, the elderly jogger may have hardening of the arteries, emphysema, or undiscovered aneurysms just waiting to burst and cause stroke or

death. Chronic arthritis in the joints will only be aggravated by persistent irritation and use. Moreover, for those of us with injuries sustained in our youth—such as torn Achilles tendons or knee cartilage—jogging might just make a painful life more painful, cancelling out the benefits the exercise is intended to produce.

(2) Jogging is a sporting activity that exercises all the main muscle groups of the body. That the arms, legs, buttocks, and torso voluntary muscles are engaged goes without question. Running down a path makes you move your upper body as well as your lower body muscles. People do not often take into account, however, how the involuntary muscle system is also put through its paces. The heart, diaphragm, and even the eye and facial muscles take part as we hurl our bodies through space at speeds up to five miles per hour over distances as long as twenty-six miles and more for some.

(3) It seems to me that jogging styles are as identifiable as fingerprints! People seem to be as individual in the way they run as they are in personality. Here comes the Duck, waddling down the track, little wings going twice as fast as the feet in an effort to stay upright. At about the quarter-mile mark, I see the Penguin, quite natty in the latest jogging suit, body stiff as a board from neck to ankles and the ankles flexing a mile a minute to cover the yards. And down there at the half-mile post—there goes the Giraffe—a tall fellow in a spotted electric yellow outfit, whose long strides cover about a dozen yards each, and whose neck waves around under some old army camouflage hat that may have served its time in a surplus store in the Bronx or in the Arabian desert. If you see the animals in the jogger woods once, you can identify them from miles away just by seeing their gait. And, by the way, be careful whose hoof you're stepping on: It may be mine!

In paragraph (1) the writer makes a statement that a number of people would debate and which isn't clearly demonstrated by science or considered common knowledge. In fact, common wisdom usually maintains the opposite thesis. Many would say that jogging improves the health of the aging—even to the point of slowing the aging process. As soon as you see a writer point to or identify an issue open to debate that stands in need of proof, he or she is setting out to persuade you that one side or the other is the more justified position. You'll notice, too, that the writer in this case takes a stand here. It's almost as if he or she is saying, "I have concluded that. . . ." But a thesis or arguable idea is only a hypothesis until evidence is summoned by the writer to prove it. Effective arguments are based on serious, factual, or demonstrable evidence, not merely opinion.

In paragraph (2) the writer is stating a fact. This is not a matter for debate. From here, the writer's evidence is to *explain* and *describe* what is meant by the fact. This is accomplished by *analyzing* (breaking down into its constituent elements) the way the different muscle groups come into play or do work when jogging, thus explaining the fact stated as a main point in the opening sentence. The assertion that jogging exercises all the muscle groups is not in question or a matter of debate. Besides taking the form of explaining how something works or what parts it comprises (for example, the basic parts of a bicycle are . . .), writers may show how the idea, object, or event functions. A writer may use this information to prove something. But if the writer doesn't argue to prove a debatable point one way or the other, then the purpose must be either to inform (as here) or to entertain.

In paragraph (3) the writer is taking a stand, but not attempting to prove anything. The paragraph is a lighthearted observation and nothing more. In addition, all of the examples used to support the statement are fanciful, funny, odd, or peculiar to the writer's particular vision. These statements are examples of figurative speech since the writer is using animal charateristics to describe joggers' running styles. Joggers aren't really animals, after all.

Make sure to examine all the facts that the author uses to support the main idea. This will allow you to decide whether or not the writer has made a case, and what sort of purpose it supports. Look for supporting details—facts, examples, illustrations, the testimony or research of experts—that are relevant to the topic in question and show what the writer says is so. In fact, paragraphs and theses consist of show and tell. The writer tells you something is so or not so and then shows you facts, illustrations, expert testimony, or experiences to back up whatever is assertedly the case or is not the case. As you determine where the author's supporting details are, you may want to label them with an "S" so that you can refer back to them easily when answering questions.

It is also important for you to be able to recognize the difference between the statements of fact presented versus statements of the author's opinion. You will be tested on this skill in this section of the test. Look at the following examples. In each case ask yourself whether you are reading a fact or an opinion.

1. Some roses are red.

2. Roses are the most beautiful flowers on Earth.

3. Everything is coming up roses.

4. Roses are the worst plants to grow in your backyard.

Item 1 is a fact. All you have to do is look at the evidence. Go to a florist. You will see that item 1 is true. A fact is anything that can be demonstrated to be objectively true in reality or which has been demonstrated to be true in reality and is documented by others. For example, the moon is orbiting about 250,000 miles from the Earth.

Item 2 is an opinion. The writer claims this as truth, but since it is a subjective quality (beauty), it remains to be seen. Others may hold different opinions. This is a matter of taste, not fact.

Item 3 is figurative language. It uses a well-known phrase to imply life is good and could not be better.

Item 4, though perhaps sometimes true, is nevertheless a matter of opinion. Many variables contribute to the health of a plant in a garden: soil, temperature range, amount of moisture, and number and kinds of bugs. This is a debatable point for which the writer would have to provide evidence.

As you read, you should note the structure of the passage. There are several common structures for the passages. Some of these structures are described below.

Main Types of Paragraph Structures

1. The structure is a main idea plus supporting arguments.

2. The structure is a main idea plus examples.

3. The structure includes comparisons or contrasts.

4. There is a pro and a con structure.

5. The structure is chronological.

6. The structure has several different aspects of one idea.

For example, a passage on education in the United States in the 1600s and 1700s might first define education, then describe colonial education, then give information about separation of church and state, and then outline the opposing and supporting arguments regarding taxation as a source of educational funding.

Being able to recognize these structures will help you recognize how the author has organized the passage. Examining the structure of the passage will help you answer questions about how the information in the text is organized and also how to summarize the information presented in the passage.

If you see a writer using a transitional pattern that reflects a sequence moving forward in time, such as "In 1982 . . . Then, in the next five years . . . A decade later, in 1997, the . . . ," chances are the writer is telling a story, describing history, or the like. Writers often use transitions of classification to analyze an idea, object, or event. They may say something like, "The first part . . . Second . . . Third . . . Finally . . ." You may then ask yourself what the analysis is for. Is it to explain or to persuade you of something? These transitional patterns may also help reveal the relationship of one part of a passage to another. For example, a writer may be writing, "On the one hand. . . . On the other hand . . ." This should alert you to the fact that the writer is comparing two things or contrasting them. What for? Is one better than the other? Worse?

By understanding the relationship among the main point, transitions, and supporting information, you may determine more readily the pattern of organization as well as the writer's purpose in a given piece of writing.

As with the paragraph examples above showing the difference among possible purposes, you must look at the relationship between the facts or information presented ("show") and what the writer is trying to point out to you ("tell") with that data. For example, the information given earlier in the paragraphs about jogging, the writer's purpose was:

(1) to persuade the audience (fact and author's opinion to persuade)

(2) to state the facts (fact with no opinion)

(3) to take a stand with no proof (opinion with no attempt to persuade)

To understand the author's purpose, the main point and the evidence that supports it must be considered together. To be meaningful, a controlling or main point is needed. You need to know if the main point is missing. You need to be able to distinguish between the writer showing data and the writer making a point.

In the two paragraphs that follow, consider the different relationship between the same data above and the controlling statement, and how that controlling statement changes the discussion from explanation to argument.

(A) Colonial education was different than today's education and consisted of several elements. Education in those days meant primarily studying the three "R's" (Reading, 'Riting, and 'Rithmetic ([colloquial language]) and the Bible. The church and state were more closely aligned with one another—education was, after all, for the purpose of serving God better, not to make more money.

(B) Colonial "education" was really just a way to create a captive audience for churches. Education in those days meant studying the three "R's" in order to learn God's word—the Bible—not commerce. The churches and the state were closely aligned with one another, and what was good for the church was good for the state—or else you were excommunicated, which kept you out of Heaven for sure.

The same informational areas are brought up in both cases, but in (A) the writer treats it more analytically ("consisted of several elements"), not taking as debatable a stand on the issue. However, the controlling statement in (B) puts forth a more volatile hypothesis, and then uses the same information to support that hypothesis.

STEP 3: REVIEW THE PASSAGE

After you finish reading actively, take ten or twenty seconds to look over the main idea and the topic sentences that you have underlined, and the key words and phrases you have marked. Now you are ready to enter Step 4 and answer the questions.

STEP 4: ANSWER THE QUESTIONS

In Step 2, you gathered enough information from the passage to answer questions dealing with main idea, purpose, support, fact vs. opinion, organization, and summarization. Let's look again at the questions from the passage on the Supreme Court.

Main Idea Questions

Looking back at the questions that follow the passage, you should see that question 1 is a main idea question.

1. The main idea of the passage is best stated in which of the following?

   (A) The Supreme Court has difficulty convicting those who violate obscenity laws.

   (B) The current definitions for obscenity and pornography provided by the Supreme Court are unworkable.

   (C) Fact-pattern analysis is insufficient for determining the attitude of the Court toward the issues of obscenity and pornography.

   (D) Despite the difficulties presented by fact-pattern analysis, Justice Segal found the solution in the patterns of search and seizure decisions.

In answering the question, you see that answer choice (C) is correct. The writer uses the second, third, fourth, and fifth paragraphs to show how fact-pattern analysis is an ineffective determinant of the Supreme Court's attitudes toward obscenity and pornography.

Choice (A) is incorrect. Nothing is ever said directly about convicting persons accused of obscenity, only that the Court has difficulty defining it.

Choice (B) is also incorrect. Though the writer states it as a fact, it is only used as an effect that leads the writer to examine how fact-pattern analysis does or does not work to reveal the "cause" or attitude of the Court toward obscenity and pornography.

Also, answer choice (D) is incorrect. The statement is contrary to what Segal found when he examined search and seizure cases.

Purpose Questions

In examining question 2, you see that you must determine the author's purpose in writing the passage.

2. The main purpose of the writer in this passage is to

    (A) convince the reader that the Supreme Court is making decisions about obscenity based on their subjective views alone.

    (B) explain to the reader how fact-pattern analysis works with respect to cases of obscenity and pornography.

    (C) define obscenity and pornography for the layperson.

    (D) demonstrate the role fact-pattern analysis plays in determining the Supreme Court's attitude about cases in obscenity and pornography.

Looking at the answer choices, you should see that choice (D) is correct. Though the writer never states it directly, the data is consistently summoned to show that fact-pattern analysis only gives us part of the picture, or "broad strokes" about the Court's attitude, but cannot account for the attitude toward individual cases.

Choice (A) is incorrect. The writer doesn't try to convince us of this fact, but merely states it as an opinion resulting from the evidence derived from the "well-documented" background of the problem.

(B) is also incorrect. The writer not only explains the role of fact-pattern analysis but also rather shows how it cannot fully apply.

The passage is about the Court's difficulty in defining obscenity and pornography. It is not an attempt to define these words for the average citizen. Nowhere do definitions for these terms appear. Therefore, choice (C) is incorrect.

Support Questions

Question 3 requires you to analyze the author's supporting details.

3. Of the following, which fact best supports the writer's contention that the Court's decisions in the areas of obscenity and pornography deserve closer scrutiny?

    (A) The fact that a Supreme Court Justice said, "I know it when I see it."

    (B) Recent studies that employ fact-pattern analysis in modeling the Court's decision-making process.

    (C) The fact that attitudes do not operate in a vacuum.

    (D) The fact that federal and state governments, interested groups, and the academic community have shown renewed interest in the obscenity and pornography decisions by the Supreme Court.

Look at the answer choices to answer this question. Choice (D) must be correct. In the fifth paragraph, the writer states that the "renewed interest"—a real and observable fact—from these groups "indicates the Court's decisions . . . deserve closer examination," another way of saying scrutiny.

Choice (A) is incorrect. The writer uses this remark to show how the Court cannot effectively define obscenity and pornography, relying on "subjective preferences" to resolve issues. The use of "I know it when I see it" is also an example of colloquial language.

In addition, choice (B) is incorrect because the writer points to the data in (D), not fact-pattern analyses, to prove this. (C), too, is incorrect. Although it is true, the writer makes this point to show how fact-pattern analysis doesn't help clear up the real-world situations in which the Court must make its decisions.

Fact vs. Opinion Questions

By examining question 4, you can see that you are required to know the difference between fact and opinion.

4. Among the following statements, which states an opinion expressed by the writer rather than a fact?

    (A) It is well documented that the area of obscenity and pornography is a difficult one for the Supreme Court.

    (B) The objects to which a court directs its attitudes are the litigants.

    (C) In many specific issue areas, the cases present strikingly similar fact-patterns.

    (D) The Court's subsequent behavior may suggest how the Court will react in other legal areas.

Keeping in mind that an opinion is something that is yet to be proven to be the case, you can determine that choice (D) is correct. It is the only statement among the four for which evidence is yet to be gathered. It is the writer's opinion that this may be a way to predict the Court's attitudes.

(A), (B), and (C) are all derived from verifiable data or documentation and are therefore incorrect.

Organization Questions

Question 5 asks you to organize given topics to reflect the organization of the passage.

5. The group of topics in the list that follows that best reflects the organization of the topics of the passage is

    (A) I.   The difficulties of the Supreme Court
         II. Several recent studies
         III. Spaeth's definition of *attitude*
         IV. The similar patterns of cases
         V.   Other issue areas
         VI. The case of *Miller v. California*

(B) I. The Supreme Court, obscenity, and fact-pattern analysis
   II. Fact-pattern analyses and attitude theory
   III. The definition of *attitude* for the Court
   IV. The definition of *situation*
   V. The breakdown in fact-pattern analysis
   VI. Studying Court behavior

(C) I. Justice Stewart's view of pornography
   II. Theoretical underpinnings
   III. A minimum-winning coalition
   IV. Search and seizure decisions
   V. Renewed interest in obscenity and pornography
   VI. The importance of local community standards

(D) I. The Court's numerous attempts to define obscenity
   II. Case characteristics
   III. The subject matter of cases
   IV. The Court's proportion of decisions
   V. Broad-based factors
   VI. Obscenity determination

After examining all of the choices, you will determine that choice (B) is the correct response. These topical areas lead directly to the implied thesis that the "role" of fact-pattern analysis is insufficient to determine the attitude of the Supreme Court in the areas of obscenity and pornography.

Choice (A) is incorrect because the first topic stated in the list is not the topic of the first paragraph. It is too global. The first paragraph is about the difficulties the Court has with defining obscenity and how fact-pattern analysis might be used to determine the Court's attitude and clear up the problem.

(C) is incorrect because each of the items listed in this topic list represents supporting evidence or data for the real topic of each paragraph. (See the list in (B) for correct topics.) For example, Justice Stewart's statement about pornography is only cited to indicate the nature of the problem the Court has with obscenity. It is not the focus of the paragraph itself.

Finally, (D) is incorrect. As with choice (C), these are all incidental pieces of information or data used to support broader points.

Summarization Questions

To answer question 6, you must be able to summarize the passage.

6.   Which paragraph among those that follow is the best summary of the passage?

(A)   The Supreme Court's decision-making process with respect to obscenity and pornography has become too subjective. Fact-pattern analyses used to determine the overall attitude of the Court reveal only broad-based attitudes on the part of the Court toward the situations of obscenity cases. But these patterns cannot fully account for the Court's attitudes toward case content. Research is not conclusive on whether fact-pattern analyses work when applied to legal areas. Renewed public and local interest suggests continued study and close examination of how the Court makes decisions. Delegating authority to the states may reflect patterns for Court decisions in other socially sensitive areas.

(B)   Though subjective, the Supreme Court decisions are well documented. Fact-pattern analyses reveal the attitude of the Supreme Court toward its decisions in cases. Spaeth explains that an attitude involves both an object and a situation. For the Court, the situation may be defined as the decision to grant certiorari. Cases present strikingly similar patterns, and a small number of variables explain a high proportion of the Court's decisions. Segal has made an effort to verify the applicability of fact-pattern analysis with some success. The Court's decisions on obscenity and pornography suggest weak Court behavior, such as in *Miller v. California*.

(C)   To determine what obscenity and pornography mean to the Supreme Court, we must use fact-pattern analysis. Fact-pattern analysis reveals the ideas that the Court uses to operate in a vacuum. The litigants and the subject matter of cases are defined in broad terms (such as an entire area of law) to reveal the Court's decision-making process. Search and seizure cases reveal strikingly similar patterns, leaving the Court open to grant certiorari effectively. Renewed public interest in the Court's decisions proves how the Court will react in the future.

(D)   Supreme Court decisions about pornography and obscenity are under examination and are out of control. The Court has to see the case to know it. Fact-pattern analyses reveal that the Court can only define cases in narrow terms, thus revealing individual egotism on the part of the Justices. As a result of strikingly similar patterns in search and seizure cases, the Court should be studied further for its weakness in delegating authority to state courts, as in the case of *Miller v. California*.

The paragraph that best and most accurately reports what the writer demonstrated based on the implied thesis is answer choice (C), which is correct.

Choice (A) is incorrect because, while it reflects some of the evidence presented in the passage, the passage does not imply that all Court decisions are subjective, just the ones about pornography and obscenity. Similarly, the writer does not suggest that ceding authority to the states (as in *Miller v. California*) is a sign of some weakness, but merely that it is worthy of study as a tool for predicting or identifying the Court's attitudes.

Response (B) is also incorrect. The writer summons information over and over to show how fact-pattern analysis cannot pin down the Court's attitude toward case content.

(D) is incorrect. Nowhere does the writer say or suggest that the justice system is "out of control" or that the justices are "egotists," only that they are liable to be reduced to being "subjective" rather than having a cogent and identifiable shared standard.

At this point, the three remaining question types must be discussed: recall questions (see question 7), cause/effect questions (see question 8), and definition questions (question 9). They are as follows.

Recall Questions

To answer question 7, you must be able to recall information from the passage.

7. Based on the passage, the rationale for fact-pattern analyses arises out of what theoretical groundwork?

   (A) Subjectivity theory

   (B) The study of cultural norms

   (C) Attitude theory

   (D) Cybernetics

The easiest way to answer this question is to refer back to the passage. In the second paragraph, the writer states that recent studies using fact-pattern analyses "owe their theoretical underpinnings to attitude theory." Therefore, we can conclude that response (C) is correct.

Answer choices (A), (B), and (D) are incorrect because they are never discussed or mentioned by the writer.

Cause/Effect Questions

Question 8 requires you to analyze a cause-and-effect relationship.

8. Based on data in the passage, what would most likely be the major cause for the difficulty in pinning down the Supreme Court's attitude toward cases of obscenity and pornography?

   (A) The personal opinions of the Court Justices

   (B) The broad nature of the situations of the cases

   (C) The ineffective logistics of certiorari

   (D) The inability of the Court to resolve the variables presented by individual case content

Choice (D) is correct, as it is precisely what fact-pattern analyses cannot resolve.

Response (A) is incorrect because no evidence is presented for it; all that is mentioned is that they do make personal decisions. Answer choice (B) is incorrect because it is one way in which fact-pattern analysis can be helpful. Finally, (C) is only a statement about certiorari being difficult to administer, and this was never claimed about them by the writer in the first place.

Definition Questions

Returning to question 9, we can now determine an answer.

9. In the context of the passage, *subjective* might be most nearly defined as

    (A) personal.

    (B) wrong.

    (C) focused.

    (D) objective.

Choice (A) is best. By taking in and noting the example of Justice Stewart provided by the writer, we can see that Justice Stewart's comment is not an example of right or wrong. Most of the time, if we are talking about people's "preferences," they are usually about taste or quality, and they are usually not a result of scientific study or clear reasoning, but arise out of personal taste, idiosyncratic intuitions, et cetera. Thus, (A) is the most likely choice.

(C) is incorrect because the Court's focus is already in place on obscenity and pornography. Choice (B) is incorrect. Nothing is implied or stated about the tightness or wrongness of the decisions themselves. Rather it is the definition of obscenity that seems "unworkable." (D) is also incorrect. *Objective* is an antonym of *subjective* in this context. To reason based on the object of study is the opposite of reasoning based upon the beliefs, opinions, or ideas of the one viewing the object, rather than the evidence presented by the object itself, independent of the observer.

You may not have been familiar with the word *subjective*, but from your understanding of the writer's intent, you should have been able to figure out what was being sought. Surrounding words and phrases almost always offer you some clues in determining the meaning of a word. In addition, any examples that appear in the text may also provide some hints.

Conclusion/Solution Questions

Let's now look at questions 10 and 11, which ask you to draw a conclusion or find a solution.

10. If you were a judge, what would be a solution that would assist in deciding obscenity and pornography cases?

    (A) Administer a fact-pattern analysis to gather data on every obscenity and pornography case.

    (B) Define the legal terms of *obscenity* and *pornography*.

    (C) Continue to look at each obscenity and pornography case individually, taking into account the Court's subjectivity.

    (D) Control case content with broad definitions of obscenity and pornography.

Choice (C) is the best response to the question because it allows individual case content to be considered when making decisions. Choice (A) is incorrect because fact-pattern analysis gathers data related to thoughts and attitudes used to make decisions. Choice (B) is incorrect because a broad definition does not allow for individual attitudes and opinions. Choice (D) is incorrect because, when used in the broad sense, it poses issues with specific cases.

11. Which of the following offers a valid conclusion a reader may reach after reading the passage?

    (A) The Supreme Court functions in a vacuum.

    (B) Popular case content affects patterns in Court decisions.

(C)   The Supreme Court intends to define the terms of *obscenity* and *pornography*.

(D)   A change in the makeup of the Supreme Court Justices could effect the decisions made on obscenity and pornography cases.

Choice (D) is a valid conclusion due to the fact that the court's decision making is subjective and depends on the justice's attitudes and opinions. Choice (A) is incorrect because attitudes and opinions play a role in the Court's decision making. Choice (B) is incorrect because the author states, "Segal found that a relatively small number of situational and case characteristic variables explain a high proportion of the Court's decisions." Choice (C) is incorrect due to studies examining Court action in previous cases that shows each case needs to be looked at individually.

INTERPRETATION OF GRAPHIC INFORMATION QUESTIONS

Graphs, charts, and tables may play a large part on the TAP, and you should be familiar with them. More than likely, you will encounter at least one passage that is accompanied by some form of graphic information. You will then be required to answer any question(s) based on the interpretation of the information presented in the graph, chart, or table.

Graphs are used to produce visual aids for sets of information. Often, the impact of numbers and statistics is diminished by an overabundance of tedious numbers. A graph helps a reader rapidly visualize or organize irregular information, as well as trace long periods of decline or increase. The following is a guide to reading the three principal graphic forms that you will encounter when taking the exam.

LINE GRAPHS

**Immigration to the United States, 1920–1930
(in Millions)**

Source: Immigration and Naturalization Service of the U.S. Dept. of Justice

Line graphs are used to track multiple elements of one or more subjects. One element is usually a time factor, over whose span the other element increases, decreases, or remains static. The lines that compose such graphs are connected points that are displayed on the chart through each integral stage. For an example, refer to the preceding immigration graph.

The average number of immigrants from 1820 to 1830 is represented at one point; the average number of immigrants from 1831 to 1840 is represented at the next. The line that connects these points is used only to ease the visual gradation between the points. It is not meant to give a strictly accurate representation for every year between the two decades. If this were so, the line would hardly be straight, even progression from year to year. The sharp directness of the lines reveals otherwise. The purpose of the graph is to plot the average increases or decreases from point to point. When dealing with more than one subject, a line graph must use either differently colored lines (or different types of lines if the graph is black-and-white). In the graph, the dark bold line represents immigration from northwestern Europe; the broken line represents immigration from southeastern Europe.

To read a line graph, find the point of change that interests you. For example, if you want to trace immigration from northwestern Europe from 1861 to 1870, you would find the position of the dark line on that point. Next, trace the position to the vertical information on the chart. In this instance, one would discover that approximately 2 million immigrants arrived from northwestern Europe in the period of time from 1861 to 1870. If wishing to discover when the number of immigrants reached 4 million, you would read across from 4 million on the vertical side of the graph, and see that this number was reached in 1881–1890 from northwestern Europe, and somewhere over the two decades from 1891 to 1910 from southeastern Europe.

BAR GRAPHS

Bar graphs are also used to plot two dynamic elements of a subject. However, unlike a line graph, the bar graph usually deals with only one subject. The exception to this is when the graph is three-dimensional, and the bars take on the dimension of depth. However, because we will be dealing only with two-dimensional graphs, we will be working only with a single subject. The other difference between a line and a bar graph is that a bar graph usually calls for a single element to be traced in terms of another, whereas a line graph usually plots either of the two elements with equal interest. For example, in the following bar graph, inflation and deflation are being marked over a span of years.

Inflation is a rise in the general level of prices. Deflation is a decline in the general level of prices. Percentage points are assigned to each year's level of prices, and that percentage decreases (deflation) from 1980 to 1981, and from 1981 to 1982. The price level is static from 1982 to 1983. The price level then increases (inflation) from 1983 to 1984. Therefore, it is obvious that the bar graph is read strictly in terms of the changes exhibited over a period of time or against some other element. Conversely, a line graph is used to plot two dynamic elements of equal interest to the reader (e.g., either number of immigrants or the particular decade in question).

To read a bar graph, simply begin with the element at the base of a bar and trace the bar to its full length. Once reaching its length, cross-reference the other element of information that matches the length of the bar.

PIE CHARTS

Pie charts differ greatly from line or bar graphs. Pie charts are used to help a reader visualize percentages of information with many elements to the subject. An entire "pie" represents 100 percent of a given quantity of information. The pie is then sliced into measurements that correspond to their respective shares of the 100 percent. For example, in the pie chart that follows, Myrna's rent occupies a slice greater than any other in the pie, because no other element equals or exceeds 25 percent of Myrna's monthly budget.

Myrna's Monthly Budget

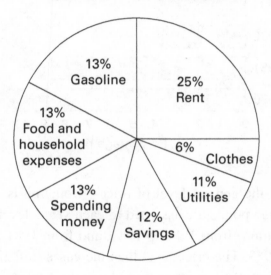

Another aspect of pie charts is that the smaller-percentage elements are arranged in consecutive order from smallest element to largest element. Therefore, the largest element in the chart will necessarily be adjacent to the smallest element in the chart, and the line that separates them is the beginning or endpoint of the chart.

To read a pie chart, choose the element of the subject that interests you and compare its size to those of the other elements. In cases where the elements are similar in size, do not assume that they are equal. The exact percentage of the element should be listed within that slice of the chart. For example, Myrna's utilities, savings, and spending money are all similar in size, but it is clear when reading the chart that each possesses a different value.

READING TABLES

Tables are useful because they relate to large bodies of information within a confined area. To read a table, cross-reference the column headings that run horizontally across the top of the table with the row headings that run vertically down the left side of the table. Scanning the table for the overall information within is usually done by reading line by line, as if reading regular text, while referring to the appropriate headings of the table to interpret the information listed. Note that some tables possess horizontal subheadings, which further ease the separation of different areas of information.

Effects of Common Drugs

Drug	Psychological Dependence	Physical Dependence	Physical Withdrawal Effects	Development of Tolerance
Depressants				
Alcohol	Mild to very strong	Very strong	Severe/dangerous	Minimal
Barbiturates	Develops slowly	Develops slowly	Death possible	Minimal
Narcotics				
Opiates (heroin, morphine)	Very strong Develops rapidly	Rapid/increases with dosage	Frightening symptoms but not dangerous	Very high; goes down quickly after withdrawal (danger if user returns to original dose)
Stimulants				
Amphetamines	Strong	Not in formal sense, but body seeks "rush"	Mild	Extremely high
Cocaine	Very strong	None	None (can cause heart spasms and instant death even if healthy)	None
Crack	Strong	Strong	Mild	High
Psychedelics				
LSD	Unpredictable	None	None	Extremely high
Marijuana	Mild to strong	Some, in high doses	None	None (some to high doses)

To use the preceding table, one should simply choose a particular drug, and then find the appropriate information needed about that drug through the headings listed at the top of the table. For example, the physical withdrawal effects of amphetamines, a stimulant drug, are mild in effect.

HELPFUL HINTS

You should approach any graphic information you encounter as a key to a larger body of information in abbreviated form. Be sure to use the visual aids of the graphics (e.g., the size of slices on pie charts) as aids only; do not ignore the written information listed on the graph, table, et cetera.

Note especially the title and headings so that you know exactly what it is at which you are looking. Also, be aware of the source of the information, where applicable. Know what each element of the graphic information represents; this will help you compare how drastic or subtle any changes are, and over what span of time they take place. Be sure you realize what the actual numbers represent, whether it is dollars, so many thousands of people, millions of shares, and so forth. Finally, note the way in which the graphic information relates to the text it seeks to illustrate; know in what ways the graphic information supports the arguments of the author of the given passage.

Language Arts

The language arts portion of the Test of Academic Proficiency asks the test-taker to use skills in the areas of grammar and composition. The objectives for this section of the test are to recognize correct and incorrect grammar and usage and to identify good and bad features of various kinds of writing.

Test-takers will be asked to read a passage and answer questions about the words or punctuation included in that passage. You may also be asked to fill in a blank with a sentence or phrase that makes the passage more effective. When taking the test, you should first skip ahead to read the questions about the particular passage. This will provide you with an idea of what to look for and focus on as you are reading. It is also important that you understand the passage as a whole and comprehend its overall intention, meaning, and/or main idea.

This chapter was developed to prepare you for the language arts section of the Test of Academic Proficiency. You will be guided through a step-by-step process for how to approach the reading passages and questions. Also included are tips to help you quickly and accurately answer the questions. By studying this review, you will greatly enhance your chances of achieving a good score on the language arts section of the Test of Academic Proficiency.

To help you master these skills, examples of the types of questions you will encounter and explanations of how to answer them are included. Even if you feel confident that you will perform well on this section, be sure to complete the example questions, as they will help sharpen your skills.

This chapter contains review material that is aligned with the Test of Academic Proficiency Standards 7 through 12. The next chapter, Chapter 4: Writing, will address the essay you will have to compose for the test's writing assignment and will help you prepare to meet Standard 13 of the Language Arts portion of the test.

A. Grammar and Usage

Standard 7   **Demonstrate command of standard usage in edited English in the United States.**

The following are examples of content that may be covered under this standard.

7.1   Understand the standard use of verbs (e.g., subject-verb agreement, verb tense, consistency of tense).

7.2   Identify and apply the standard use of pronouns (e.g., pronoun-antecedent agreement, standard pronoun case, use of possessive pronouns, standard use of relative and demonstrative pronouns).

7.3   Recognize and apply the standard use of modifiers (e.g., adverbs, adjectives, prepositional phrases).

Standard 8   **Understand and apply knowledge of mechanical conventions in edited English in the United States.**

The following are examples of content that may be covered under this standard.

8.1   Recognize instances in which incorrect or extraneous punctuation has been used or necessary punctuation has been omitted.

8.2   Identify standard initial capitalization and standard capitalization with proper words and titles.

8.3   Recognize the standard spelling of words.

B. Writing

Standard 9 **Understand the role of purpose and audience in written communication.**

The following are examples of content that may be covered under this standard.

9.1   Assess the appropriateness of written material for a specific purpose or audience (e.g., a business letter, a communication to parents).

9.2   Determine the likely effect on an audience of a writer's choice of a particular word or words (e.g., to evoke sympathy, to raise questions about an opposing point of view).

9.3   Identify persuasive techniques used by a writer in a passage.

9.4   Demonstrate the ability to adapt forms, organizational strategies, and styles for different audiences and purposes.

Standard 10 **Understand unity, focus, development, and organization in writing.**

The following are examples of content that may be covered under this standard.

10.1   Identify organizational methods used by the author of a passage.

10.2   Distinguish between effective and ineffective thesis statements.

10.3   Recognize unnecessary shifts in point of view (e.g., shifts from first to third person) or distracting details that impair development of the main idea in a passage.

10.4   Select appropriate and effective supporting material.

10.5   Recognize examples of focused, concise, and well-developed writing.

Standard 11 **Understand and apply editing and revision strategies.**

The following are examples of content that may be covered under this standard.

11.1   Apply editing and revision strategies affecting diction, syntax, transitions, organization, clarity, coherence, and point of view.

11.2 Make revisions that improve the unity and focus of a passage or that improve cohesion and the effective sequence of ideas.

11.3 Improve the clarity and effectiveness of a passage through changes in word choice.

11.4 Eliminate or replace unnecessary or imprecise words and phrases.

11.5 Insert appropriate transitional words or phrases (e.g., *however, as a result*) in a passage to convey the structure of the text and to help readers understand the sequence of a writer's ideas.

Standard 12 **Recognize sentences and paragraphs that effectively communicate intended messages.**

The following are examples of content that may be covered under this standard.

12.1 Demonstrate an understanding of unity within paragraphs and apply methods for enhancing paragraph organization and unity.

12.2 Recognize effective topic sentences and distinguish between effective and ineffective development of ideas within a paragraph.

12.3 Identify sentence fragments and run-on sentences.

12.4 Recognize wordiness, redundancy, and ineffective repetition in sentences and paragraphs.

12.5 Recognize inefficiency in sentence and paragraph construction.

THE READING PASSAGES

The reading passages in this section are designed for a wide range of audiences. As a result, the readings will address an array of diverse subjects. Although you will not be expected to have prior knowledge of the information presented in the passages, you will be expected to know the fundamental writing techniques needed to convey the passage's message to its intended audience. Only your ability to write standard English for a specific audience will be tested. For example, you may encounter a passage such as the following one, written for a high school history textbook:

[1]After the Civil War, raw cotton regained its traditional role as America's largest export good. [2]From 1803 to 1937, the Civil War and two other years excluded, unprocessed cotton was America's largest merchandise export. [3]The United States was also an important exporter of grain and mineral products. [4]What most characterized the growth of American exports in the late nineteenth century, _____, was the rise of manufactured goods exports: refined petroleum, machinery, and other manufactured goods. [5]Most of these goods were mass-produced products made by methods that were not used abroad, such as sewing machines, harvesters, and, later, automobiles. [6]Exports, increased rapidly, as American goods became highly competitive in world markets.

[7]Exports rose even faster than imports, with the consequence that exports always exceeded imports until 1971. [8]When the balance of trade remained consistently positive, Americans gradually recognized that a high tariff policy was no longer necessary or even desirable. [9]In 1913, with traditionally low-tariff Democrats in control of Congress, the Underwood Tariff lowered duties substantially. [10]International commerce expanded faster in the late nineteenth and early twentieth centuries than did worldwide output, with the gold standard aiding in this growth.

THE QUESTIONS

Each passage will be followed by a number of questions. Some questions may require you to find mistakes in standard English usage, while others may ask you to supply appropriate words or phrases in blanks. You will commonly encounter questions that will ask you to do the following:

- Identify the incorrect use of words.

- Identify the incorrect use of punctuation.

- Determine which sentence best makes the transition from one thought to another.

- Determine which word or phrase would be best for a specific audience.

- Determine the type of organization the author of the passage is using.

For example, questions for the passage above might be like these [correct answers are boldface]:

(Note that superscripted numbers that appear before the sentences in the passage are referred to in the questions and answers as "Part.")

1. Which of the following parts does not use standard punctuation?

   A. 2

   B. 6

   C. 8

   D. 9

2. Which of the following words used in the blank in Part 4 would make a good transition from the previous sentence?

   A. consequently

   B. moreover

   C. nevertheless

   D. however

VERBS (Standard 7)

This section covers the principal parts of some irregular verbs, including such troublesome verbs as *lie* and *lay*. The use of regular verbs, such as *look* and *receive*, poses few problems for most writers because the past and past participle forms end in *-ed*; it is the irregular forms, however, that pose the most serious challenge—for example, *seen, written,* and *begun.*

Verb Tenses

Tense sequence indicates a logical time sequence.

Use present tense:

In statements of universal truth:

I learned that the sun is ninety million miles from the Earth.

In statements about the contents of literature and other published work:

In this book, Sandy becomes a nun and writes a book about psychology.

Use past tense:

In statements or questions about action that happened in the past and is now finished:

I fell over the limb and broke my arm.

How did you break your arm?

In statements concerning writing or publication of a book:

He wrote his first book in 1949, and it was published in 1956.

Use present perfect tense:

For an action that began in the past but continues into the future:

I have lived here all my life.

Use past perfect tense:

For an earlier action that is mentioned in relation to a later action:

Shaunika ate the apple that she had picked.

(First she picked it; then she ate it.)

Use future perfect tense:

For an action that will have been completed at a specific future time:

You will have graduated by the time we next meet.

Use a present participle:

For action that occurs at the same time as the verb:

Speeding down the interstate, I saw a cop's flashing lights.

Use a perfect participle:

For action that occurred before the main verb:

Having read the directions, I started the test.

Use the subjunctive mood:

To express a wish or state a condition contrary to fact:

If it were not raining, we could have a picnic.

In "that" clauses after such verbs as *request, recommend, suggest, ask, require,* and *insist*; and after such expressions as *it is important* and *it is necessary*:

It is necessary that all papers be submitted on time.

Subject-Verb Agreement

Agreement is the grammatical correspondence between the subject and the verb of a sentence or clause: *I do; you do; we do; they do; he, she, it does.* One source of confusion for many students is which verb form is singular and which plural, so this section begins by focusing on making that distinction and then tackles the task of identifying the real subject of a sentence. This section addresses subjects that are commonly construed as singular and those that are construed as plural.

Every English verb has five forms, two of which are the bare form (plural) and the *-s* form (singular). Simply put, singular verb forms end in *-s*; plural forms do not.

Study these rules governing subject-verb agreement:

A verb must agree with its subject, not with any additional phrase in the sentence, such as a prepositional or verbal phrase.

Your *copy* of the rules *is* on the desk.

Ms. Garza's *record* of community service and outstanding teaching qualifies her for a promotion.

In an inverted sentence beginning with a prepositional phrase, the verb must still agree with its subject.

At the end of the summer *come* the best *sales*.

Under the house *are* some old Mason *jars*.

Prepositional phrases beginning with compound prepositions such as *along with*, *together with*, *in addition to*, and *as well as* should be ignored, for they do not affect subject-verb agreement.

Gladys Knight, along with the Pips, *is* riding the midnight train to Georgia.

A verb must agree with its subject, not its subject complement.

Taxes are a problem.

One *problem is* taxes.

His main *source* of pleasure *is* food and women.

Food and women are his main source of pleasure.

When a sentence begins with an expletive such as *there, here,* or *it*, the verb agrees with the subject, not the expletive.

Surely there *are* several *alumni* who would be interested in starting a group.

There *are* 50 *students* in my English class.

There *is* a horrifying *study* on child abuse in *Psychology Today*.

Indefinite pronouns such as *each, either, one, everyone, everybody,* and *everything* are singular.

> *Somebody* in Detroit *loves* me.

> *Does either* [one] of you have a pencil?

> *Neither* of my brothers *has* a car.

Indefinite pronouns such as *several, few, both,* and *many* are considered plural.

> *Both* of my sorority sisters *have* decided to live off campus.

> *Few seek* the enlightenment of transcendental meditation.

Indefinite pronouns such as *all, some, most,* and *none* may be singular or plural, depending on their referents.

> *Some* of the food *is* cold.

> *Some* of the vegetables *are* cold.

> I can think of some retorts, but *none seem* appropriate.

> *None* of the children *is* as sweet as Nina.

Fractions such as *one-half* and *one-third* may be singular or plural, depending on the referent.

> Half of the mail has been delivered.

> *Half of* the letters *have* been read.

Subjects joined by *and* take a plural verb unless the subjects are commonly thought of as one item or unit.

> *Jim and Tammy were* televangelists.

> *Guns and Roses is* my favorite group.

In cases when the subjects are joined by *or, nor, either . . .or,* or *neither . . .nor,* the verb must agree with the subject closer to it.

Either the teacher or the *students are* responsible.

Neither the students nor the *teacher is* responsible.

Relative pronouns—such as *who, which, or that*—require plural verbs if they refer to plural antecedents. However, when the relative pronoun refers to a singular subject, the pronoun takes a singular verb.

She is one of the best *cheerleaders who have* ever attended our school.

She is the only *cheerleader who has* a broken leg.

Subjects preceded by *every* and *each* are singular.

Every man, woman, and child *was* given a life preserver.

Each undergraduate *is* required to pass a proficiency exam.

A collective noun, such as *audience, faculty*, and *jury,* requires a singular verb when the group is regarded as a whole, and a plural when the members of the group are regarded as individuals.

The *jury has* made its decision.

The *faculty are* preparing their grade rosters.

Subjects preceded by *the number of* or *the percentage of* are singular; subjects preceded by *a number of* or *a percentage of* are plural.

The number of vacationers in Florida *increases* every year.

A number of vacationers *are* young couples.

Certain nouns of Latin and Greek origin have unusual plural forms.

Singular	Plural
criterion	criteria
alumnus	alumni
datum	data
medium	media

The *data are* available for inspection.

The only *criterion* for membership *is* a high GPA.

Some nouns, such as *deer, shrimp*, and *sheep*, have the same spelling for both their singular and plural forms. In these cases, the meaning of the sentence will determine whether they are singular or plural.

Deer are beautiful animals.

The spotted *deer is* licking the salt block.

Some nouns ending in *-ics*, such as *economics* and *ethics*, take singular verbs when they refer to principles or a field of study; however, when they refer to individual practices, they usually take plural verbs.

Ethics is being taught in the spring.

His unusual business *ethics are* what got him into trouble.

Some nouns that end in *-s* may appear to be plural but are not; examples are *measles* and *news*.

Measles is a very contagious disease.

News of her arrival *was* not welcome.

A verbal noun (infinitive or gerund) serving as a subject is treated as singular, even if the object of the verbal phrase is plural.

Hiding your mistakes *does* not make them go away.

A plural subject followed by a singular appositive requires a plural verb; similarly, a singular subject followed by a plural appositive requires a singular verb.

When the girls throw a party, *they* each bring a *gift*.

The *board*, all ten members, *is* meeting today.

PRONOUNS (Standard 7)

Pronoun Case

One of the most embarrassing mistakes you can make in written English is confusing the spelling of common pronouns: *its* and *it's* and *your* and *you're*. The words *its* and *your* are possessive pronouns, meaning "belonging to it" and "belonging to you," respectively. *It's* and *you're* are contractions for *it is* and *you are*.

Watch *your* step; if you don't, you might break *your* neck.

It's not likely that the company will give back *its* windfall profits.

Other commonly asked questions regarding the use of pronouns are about confusing nominative case pronouns with objective case pronouns.

Nominative Case	Objective Case
I	me
he	him
she	her
we	us
they	them
who	whom

Use the **nominative case** (subject of pronouns) in the following:

Subject of a sentence:

We studied until early morning.

Alan and *I* "burned the midnight oil" too.

Pronouns in apposition to the subject:

Only two students, Alex and *I*, were asked to comment.

Predicate nominative/subject complement:

The cast members nominated for the award were *she* and *I*.

The subject of a subordinate clause:

Robert is the driver *who* reported the accident.

The only pronouns that are acceptable in standard English after prepositions are the objective case pronouns. When deciding between *who* and *whom* in the sentence "We're having difficulty deciding *who* we can trust," try substituting *he* for *who* and *him* for *whom*; then follow these transformation steps:

1. Isolate the *who* or *whom* clause: who we can trust.

2. Invert the natural word order if necessary, to the normal English subject–verb order: we can trust who

3. Read the final form with the *he* or *him* inserted: we can trust ~~who~~ *him*. The correct pronoun is thus *whom*.

Use the objective case (subject of pronouns) for the following:

Direct object of a verb:

Mary invited *us* to her party.

Object of a preposition:

The torn books belonged to *her*.

Just between you and *me*, I'm bored.

Indirect object of a verb:

Soren gave *her* a dozen roses.

Appositive of an object:

The committee selected two delegates, Barbara and *me*.

Object of an infinitive:

The young boy wanted to help *us* paint the fence.

Subject of an infinitive:

The boss told *him* to work late.

Object of a gerund:

Enlisting *him* was surprisingly easy.

When a conjunction connects two pronouns or a pronoun and a noun, one good way to determine the case of a pronoun is to remove the *and* and the noun or other pronoun:

Mom gave ~~Tom and~~ myself a piece of cake.

Mom gave ~~Tom and~~ I a piece of cake.

Mom gave ~~Tom and~~ me a piece of cake.

Removal of the crossed-out words reveals that the correct pronoun should be *me*.

Pronoun-Antecedent Agreement

Some questions might ask you about *pronoun-antecedent agreement*. These kinds of questions test your knowledge of using an appropriate pronoun to agree with its antecedent in number (singular or plural form) and gender (masculine, feminine, or neuter). An *antecedent* is a noun or pronoun to which another noun or pronoun refers.

Here are the two basic rules for pronoun reference-antecedent agreement:

1. Every pronoun must have a conspicuous antecedent.

2. Every pronoun must agree with its antecedent in number, gender, and person.

When an antecedent is one of dual gender—such as student, singer, person, or citizen—use *his* or *her*. Some careful writers change the antecedent to a plural noun to avoid using the sexist, singular masculine pronoun.

UNREVISED:	Everyone hopes that they will win the lottery.
CORRECT BUT AMBIGUOUS:	Everyone hopes that he will win the lottery.
CORRECT BUT AWKWARD:	Everyone hopes that he or she will win the lottery.
REVISED:	Most people hope that they will win the lottery.

Ordinarily, the relative pronoun *who* is used to refer to people, *which* to refer to things and places, *where* to refer to places, and *that* to refer to places or things. The distinction between *that* and *which* is a grammatical distinction (see the section on Word Choice skills). Many writers prefer to use *that* to refer to collective nouns, even for people: A family that traces its lineage is usually proud of its roots.

Quite often, writers—especially students—are not sure when to use the reflexive case pronoun and when to use the possessive case pronoun. The rules governing the usage of the reflexive case and the possessive case are simple.

Use the possessive case:

Before a noun in a sentence:

My dog has fleas, but her dog doesn't.

Before a gerund in a sentence:

Her running helps to relieve stress.

As a noun in a sentence:

Mine was the last test graded that day.

To indicate possession:

Brad thought the book was his, but it was someone else's.

Use the reflexive case:

As a direct object to rename the subject:

I kicked myself.

As an indirect object to rename the subject:

Henry bought himself a tie.

As an object of a prepositional phrase:

Tom and Lillie baked the pie for themselves.

As a predicate pronoun:

She hasn't been herself lately.

DO NOT use the reflexive in place of the nominative pronoun:

UNREVISED: Both Randy and myself plan to go.

REVISED: Both Randy and *I* plan to go.

UNREVISED: *Yourself* will take on the challenges of college.

REVISED: *You* will take on the challenges of college *yourself*.

Watch out for careless use of the pronoun form:

UNREVISED: George hisself told me it was true.

REVISED: George *himself* told me it was true.

UNREVISED: They washed the car *theirselves*.

REVISED: They washed the car *themselves*.

Notice that reflexive pronouns are **NOT** set off by commas:

UNREVISED: Mary, *herself*, gave him the diploma.

REVISED: Mary herself gave him the diploma.

Pronoun Reference

Pronoun reference questions require you to determine whether the antecedent is conspicuously written in the sentence or whether it is remote, implied, ambiguous, or vague, none of which results in clear writing. In the following, make sure that every italicized pronoun has a conspicuous antecedent and that one pronoun substitutes only for another noun or pronoun, not for an idea or a sentence.

Pronoun reference problems occur in the following instances:

1. When a pronoun refers to either of two antecedents.

   UNREVISED: Joanna told Tina that *she* was getting fat.

   REVISED: Joanna told Tina, "I'm getting fat."

   OR

   Joanna told Tina, "You're getting fat."

2. When a pronoun refers to a nonexistent antecedent.

   UNREVISED: A strange car followed us closely, and *he* kept blinking his lights at us.

   REVISED: A strange car followed us closely, and its driver kept blinking his lights at us.

3. When *this, that*, and *which* refer to the general idea of the preceding clause or sentence rather than the preceding word.

   UNREVISED: The students could not understand the pronoun reference handout, *which* annoyed them very much.

   REVISED: The students could not understand the pronoun reference handout, a *fact that* annoyed them very much.

   OR

   The students were annoyed because they could not understand the pronoun reference handout.

4. When a pronoun refers to an unexpressed but implied noun.

   UNREVISED: My husband wants me to knit a blanket, but I'm not interested in it.

   REVISED: My husband wants me to knit a blanket, but I'm not interested in *knitting*.

5. When *it* is used as something other than an expletive to postpone a subject.

   UNREVISED: The football game was canceled because it was bad weather.

   REVISED: The football game was canceled because the weather was bad.

6. When *they* or *it* is used to refer to something or someone indefinitely, and there is no definite antecedent.

   UNREVISED: At the job placement office, they told me to stop wearing ripped jeans to my interviews.

   REVISED: At the job placement office, I was told to stop wearing ripped jeans to my interviews.

7. When the pronoun does not agree with its antecedent in number, gender, or person.

   UNREVISED: Any graduate student, if *they* are interested, may tend the lecture.

   REVISED: Any graduate student, if *he* or *she* is interested, may attend the lecture.

   REVISED: All graduate students, if *they* are interested, may attend the lecture.

ADJECTIVES AND ADVERBS (Standard 7)

Correct Usage

Be careful and *Drive carefully* are sentences that illustrate the differences that this section discusses: the proper use of an adjective or an adverb, including distinctions between *bad* and *badly* and *good* and *well*.

Adjectives are words that modify nouns or pronouns by defining, describing, limiting, or qualifying those nouns or pronouns.

Adverbs are words that modify verbs, adjectives, or other adverbs and that express such ideas as time, place, manner, cause, and degree. In general, use adjectives as subject complements with linking verbs; use adverbs with action verbs.

The old man's speech was *eloquent*.	**ADJECTIVE**
Mr. Brown speaks *eloquently*.	**ADVERB**
Please be *careful*.	**ADJECTIVE**
Please drive *carefully*.	**ADVERB**

Good and Well

Good is an adjective; its use as an adverb is colloquial and nonstandard.

NONSTANDARD:	He plays *good*.
STANDARD:	He plays *well*.
STANDARD:	He looks *good* for an octogenarian.

Well may be either an adverb or an adjective. As an adjective it means "in good health."

He plays *well*.	**ADVERB**
My mother is not *well*.	**ADJECTIVE**

Do not confuse *good* and *well* when used with *feel*. If you say "I feel good," you're referring to your general health or mood, whereas "I feel well" refers only to your sense of touch.

Bad or Badly

Bad is an adjective used after sense verbs, such as *look, smell, taste, feel,* or *sound,* or after linking verbs (*is, am, are, was, were*).

> **UNREVISED:** I feel *badly* about the delay.
>
> **REVISED:**   I feel *bad* about the delay.

Badly is an adverb used after all other verbs.

> **UNREVISED:** It doesn't hurt very *bad*.
>
> **REVISED:**   It doesn't hurt very *badly*.

Real or Really

Real is an adjective; its use as an adverb is colloquial and nonstandard. It means "genuine."

> **NONSTANDARD:** He writes *real* well.
>
> **STANDARD:**   This is *real* leather.

Really is an adverb meaning "very."

> **NONSTANDARD:** This is *really* diamond.
>
> **STANDARD:**   Have a *really* nice day.

This is *real* amethyst.	**ADJECTIVE**
This is *really* difficult.	**ADVERB**
This is a *real* crisis	**ADJECTIVE**
This is *really* important.	**ADVERB**

Faulty Comparisons

This section covers comparisons that use adjectives and adverbs with certain conjunctions, such as *than* and *as*, to indicate a greater or lesser degree of what is specified in the main part of the sentence. Errors occur when the comparison being made is illogical, redundant, or incomplete. Watch for *-er* and *-est* forms of words meaning *more* and *most*, and correlative pairs like *as . . .as*. Other clues are *than* and *other*. Often, sentences containing a faulty comparison sound correct because their problem is not one of grammar but of logic. Read such sentences closely to make sure that like things are being compared, that the comparisons are complete, and that the comparisons are logical.

When comparing two persons or things, use the comparative (*-er*), not the superlative (*-est*) form, of an adjective or an adverb. Use the superlative form for comparison of more than two persons or things. Use *any, other*, or *else* when comparing one thing or person with a group of which it, he, or she is a part.

Most one- and two-syllable words form their comparative and superlative forms with *-er* and *-est* suffixes. Adjectives and adverbs of more than two syllables form their comparatives and superlatives with the addition of *more* and *most*.

Word	Comparative	Superlative
good	better	best
old	older	oldest
friendly	friendlier	friendliest
lonely	lonelier	loneliest
talented	more talented	most talented
beautiful	more beautiful	most beautiful

When in doubt, consult a dictionary; most of them give the comparative and superlative forms.

Here are examples of some common types of faulty comparison:

Double comparison

UNREVISED: He is the *most nicest* brother.

REVISED: He is the *nicest* brother.

UNREVISED: She is the *more meaner* of the sisters.

REVISED: She is the *meaner* sister.

Illogical comparison

UNREVISED: The interest at a loan company is higher than a bank.

CORRECT: The interest at a loan company is higher *than at* a bank.

Ambiguous comparison

UNREVISED: I like Mary better than you. (than you what?)

REVISED: I like Mary better than I like you.

OR

I like Mary better than you do.

Incomplete comparison

UNREVISED: Skywriting is more spectacular.

REVISED: Skywriting is more spectacular than billboard advertising.

Omission of words *other, any*, or *else* when comparing one thing or person with a group of which it, he, or she is a part

UNREVISED: Joan writes better *than* any student in her class.

REVISED: Joan writes better *than any other* student in her class.

Omission of the second *as* in an *as . . .as* construction

UNREVISED: The University of West Florida is *as large* or larger than the University of North Florida.

REVISED: The University of West Florida is *as large as* or larger than the University of Northern Florida.

PUNCTUATION AND CAPITALIZATION (Standard 8)

Commas

Commas should be placed according to standard rules of punctuation for purpose, clarity, and effect. On the test, you will be given choices that require your knowledge of such rules. The proper use of commas is explained in the following rules and examples.

In a series:

When more than one adjective describes a noun, use a comma to separate and emphasize each adjective. The comma takes the place of the word and in the series.

> the long, dark passageway

> another confusing, sleepless night

> an elaborate, complex, brilliant plan

Some adjective-noun combinations are thought of as one word. In these cases, the adjective in front of the adjective-noun combination needs no comma. (If you were to insert **and** between the adjective-noun combination, it would not make sense.)

> a stately oak tree

> a superior elementary school

The comma is also used to separate words, phrases, and whole ideas (clauses); it still takes the place of **and** when used this way.

> a lovely lady, an elegant dress, and many admirers

> She lowered the shade, closed the curtain, turned off the light, and went to bed.

One question that exists about the use of commas in a series is whether one should be used before the final item. It is standard usage to do so, although newspapers and many magazines do not use the final comma. Occasionally, the omission of the comma can be confusing.

With a long introductory phrase:

Usually if a phrase of more than five or six words or if a dependent clause precedes the subject at the beginning of a sentence, a comma is used to set it off:

> After last night's fiasco at the disco, she couldn't bear the thought of looking at him again.

> Whenever I try to talk about politics, my wife leaves the room.

If an introductory phrase includes a verb form that is being used as another part of speech (a **verbal**), it must be followed by a comma:

> **UNREVISED:** When eating Mary never looked up from her plate.

> **REVISED:**   When eating, Mary never looked up from her plate.

> **UNREVISED:** Having decided to leave Mary James wrote her a long email.

> **REVISED:**   Having decided to leave Mary, James wrote her a long email.

To separate sentences with two main ideas:

To understand this use of the comma, you need to be able to recognize compound sentences. When a sentence contains more than two subjects and verbs (clauses), and the two clauses are joined by a coordinating conjunction (*and, but, or, nor, for, yet*), use a comma before the conjunction to show that another independent clause is coming.

> I thought I knew the poem by heart, but he showed me some lines I had forgotten.

> He is supposed to leave tomorrow, but he is not ready to go.

> Jim knows you are disappointed, and he has known it for a long time.

If the two parts of the sentence are short and closely related, it is not necessary to use a comma.

> He threw the ball and the dog ran after it.

Be careful not to confuse a sentence that has a compound verb and a single subject with a compound sentence. If the subject is the same for both verbs, there is no need for a comma.

> **UNREVISED:** Charles sent some flowers, and wrote a long note explaining why he had not been able to attend.

> **REVISED:** Charles sent some flowers and wrote a long note explaining why he had not been able to attend.

> **UNREVISED:** Last Thursday we went to the concert with Julia, and afterward dined at an old Italian restaurant.

> **REVISED:** Last Thursday we went to the concert with Julia and afterward dined at an old Italian restaurant.

In general, words and phrases that stop the flow of the sentence or are unnecessary for the main idea are set off by commas.

Abbreviations after names

> Martha Harris, Ph.D., will be the speaker tonight.

Interjections (An exclamation without added grammatical connection)

> Oh, I'm so glad to see you!

> Hey, let us out of here!

Direct address

> Roy, won't you open the door for the dog?

> Hey, lady, watch out for that car!

Tag questions

> Jerry looks like his father, doesn't he?

Geographical names and addresses

The concert will be held in Chicago, Illinois, on August 12. [Note: Punctuation must always follow a state name when that name follows a city — except in postal addresses, as illustrated in the next item.]

The letter was addressed to Mrs. Marion Heartwell, 1881 Pine Lane, Palo Alto, California 95824.

Transitional words and phrases

On the other hand, I hope he gets better.

I've always found, however, that the climate is better in the mountains.

Parenthetical words and phrases

In fact, I planted corn last summer.

The Mannes affair was, to put it mildly, a surprise.

With nonrestrictive elements:

Parts of a sentence that modify other parts are sometimes essential to the meaning of the sentence and sometimes not. When a modifying word or phrase is not vital to the meaning of the sentence, it is set off by commas. Because it does not restrict the meaning of the words it modifies, it is called nonrestrictive. Modifiers that are essential to the meaning of the sentence are restrictive; they are not set off by commas.

ESSENTIAL: The girl who wrote the story is my sister.

NONESSENTIAL: My sister, the girl who wrote the story, has always loved to write.

ESSENTIAL: The man who is wearing the red sweater is the best-dressed person in the class.

NONESSENTIAL: Jorge, who is wearing the red sweater, is the best-dressed person in the class.

To set off direct quotations:

Most direct quotes or quoted materials are set off from the rest of the sentence by commas.

> "Please read your part more loudly," the director insisted.

> "I won't know what to do," said Michael, "if you ever leave me alone."

> Who was it who said, "Do not ask for whom the bell tolls; it tolls for thee"?

Note: In American English, commas always go inside the closing quotation mark, even if the comma is not part of the material being quoted.

To set off contrasting elements.

> Her intelligence, not her beauty, got her the job.

> It was a reasonable, though not appealing, idea.

In dates:

In the month-day-year form, commas follow the day and year.

> She will arrive April 6, 2006, on the *Queen Elizabeth*.

If only the month and year are given, no commas are necessary.

> The minister's January 1967 resignation was unexpected.

The day-month-year form requires no punctuation.

> The events of 14 April 1865 were unprecedented.

Because a specific date makes a descriptive phrase following it nonessential, that phrase will be nonrestrictive and therefore set off by a comma.

> He was married on 7 October 1988, which fell five days after his forty-third birthday.

When a subordinate clause is at the end of a sentence, a comma preceding the clause is optional. However, when a subordinate clause introduces a sentence, a comma should be used after the clause. Here are some common subordinating conjunctions:

after	even though	till
although	if	unless
as	inasmuch as	until
as if	since	when
because	so that	whenever
before	though	while

Semicolons

This review section covers the basic uses of the semicolon: to separate independent clauses not joined by a coordinating conjunction, to separate independent clauses separated by a conjunctive adverb, and to separate items in a series with internal commas.

Use the semicolon in the following cases:

To separate independent clauses that are not joined by a coordinating conjunction.

I understand how to use commas; the semicolon I have yet to master.

To separate two independent clauses connected by a conjunctive adverb.

He took great care with his work; therefore, he was very successful.

Usually a comma follows the conjunctive adverb. Note also that a period can be used to separate two sentences joined by a conjunctive adverb. Here are some common conjunctive adverbs:

accordingly	indeed	now
besides	in fact	on the other hand
consequently	moreover	otherwise
finally	nevertheless	perhaps
furthermore	next	still
however	nonetheless	therefore

Then is also used as a conjunctive adverb, but it is not usually followed by a comma.

To combine two independent clauses connected by a coordinating conjunction if either or both of the clauses contain other internal punctuation:

Success in college, some maintain, requires intelligence, industry, and perseverance; but others, fewer in number, assert that only geniality is important.

To separate items in a series when each item has internal punctuation. It is important to be consistent; if you use a semicolon between any of the items in the series, you must use semicolons to separate all of the items in the series.

I bought an old, dilapidated chair; an antique table that was in beautiful condition; and a new, ugly, blue and white rug.

Do not use the semicolon in any other cases, especially as a substitute for a comma. Here are some examples of nonstandard semicolon use; all of them should be replaced with a comma:

You should never make such statements; even though they are correct.

My roommate also likes sports; particularly football, basketball, and baseball.

Being of a cynical mind; I should ask for a recount of the ballots.

Note: The semicolon is not a terminal mark of punctuation; therefore, it should not be followed by a capital letter unless the first word in the second clause ordinarily requires capitalization.

Colons

The difference between the colon and the semicolon and between the colon and the period is that the colon is an introductory mark, not a terminal mark. The colon signals the reader that a list, explanation, or restatement of the preceding thought will follow. It is like an arrow, indicating that something is to follow.

Here are some examples of colons used to introduce lists. Note that some lists may have only one item.

> I hate just one course: English.

> Three plays by William Shakespeare will be presented in repertory this summer at Illinois State: *Hamlet*, *Macbeth*, and *Othello*.

> The reasons he cited for his success are as follows: honesty, industry, and a pleasant disposition.

A colon should also be used to separate two independent clauses when the second clause is a restatement or explanation of the first:

> All of my high school teachers said one thing in particular: college would be difficult.

You should also use a colon to introduce a word or word group that is a restatement, explanation, or summary of the first sentence:

> The first week of camping was wonderful: we lived in cabins instead of tents.

In standard English the colon should only be used after statements that are grammatically complete. Do not, for example, use a colon after a verb or a preposition.

> **UNREVISED:** My favorite holidays are: Christmas, New Year's Eve, and Halloween.
>
> **REVISED:** My favorite holidays are Christmas, New Year's Eve, and Halloween.
>
> **UNREVISED:** I enjoy different ethnic dishes, such as those from: Greece, China, Provence, and Italy.
>
> **REVISED:** I enjoy different ethnic dishes, such as those from Greece, China, Provence, and Italy.

However, the use of a colon to set off a displayed list is becoming more common and may now be considered standard.

Apostrophes

Apostrophes are used to make a noun possessive, not plural. Remember the following rules when considering how to show possession:

Add 's to singular nouns and indefinite pronouns:

Tiffany's flowers

at the owner's expense

a dog's bark

Add 's to singular nouns ending in s, unless this distorts the pronunciation:

Delores's paper

the boss's pen

Dr. Yots' class or Dr. Yots's class (depending on pronunciation)

for righteousness' sake

Add an apostrophe to plural nouns ending in s or *es*:

two cents' worth

three weeks' pay

ladies' night

Add 's to plural nouns not ending in s:

men's room

children's toys

Add 's to the last word in compound words or groups:

brother-in-law's car

someone else's paper

Add *'s* to the last name when indicating joint ownership:

> Joe and Edna's home

> Ted and Jane's marriage

Add *'s* to both names if you intend to show ownership by each person:

> Joe's and Edna's trucks

> Ted's and Jane's marriage vows

Possessive pronouns change their forms without the addition of an apostrophe:

> hers, his, its, yours, theirs

Quotation Marks and Italics

The most common use of double quotation marks (") is to set off quoted words, phrases, and sentences.

> "If everybody minded their own business," said Mrs. O'Leary in a huff, "the world would be a much nicer place."

Single quotation marks are used to set off quoted material within a quote.

> "Shall I bring 'Rime of the Ancient Mariner' along with us?" asked her brother.

> "If she said that to me," Katherine insisted, "I would tell her, 'I never intend to speak to you again! Goodbye, Susan!'"

To set off titles of poems, stories, and book chapters, use quotation marks. Book, motion picture, newspaper, and magazine titles are italicized when printed.

> The article "Moving South in the Southern Rain," by Jergen Smith, appeared in the *Southern News*.

> The assignment is "Childhood Development," which is Chapter 18 of *Abnormal Behavior*.

Remember that commas and periods at the end of quotations are always placed inside the quotation marks even if they are not actually part of the quote. Semicolons and colons are always placed outside. Question marks are placed inside or outside, depending on whether the quotation is a question.

UNREVISED:	"If my dog could talk", Mary mused, "I'll bet he'd say, 'Take me for a walk right this minute'".
REVISED:	"If my dog could talk," Mary mused, "I'll bet he'd say, 'Take me for a walk right this minute.'"
UNREVISED:	She called down the stairs, "When are you going"?
REVISED:	She called down the stairs, "When are you going?"
UNREVISED:	We have to "pull ourselves up by our bootstraps;" we can't just talk about our plans.
REVISED:	We have to "pull ourselves up by our bootstraps"; we can't just talk about our plans.

Remember to use only one mark of punctuation at the end of sentence ending with a quotation mark.

UNREVISED:	She thought out loud, "Will I ever finish this project in time for that class?".
REVISED:	She thought out loud, "Will I ever finish this project in time for that class?"

Capitalization

There are many conventions for beginning words with capital letters; this section will review just a few of the more common ones. In general, capitalize (1) all proper nouns and adjectives, (2) the first word of a sentence, and (3) the first word of a direct quotation. Points (2) and (3) are easy to figure out, but knowing which nouns and adjectives are "proper" is sometimes difficult. Here is a brief list that will help you remember what words to capitalize.

Names of persons, geographical places, and organizations:

Kelvim Escobar was a pitcher for the Anaheim Angels, who play in the American League.

Titles of books, poems, songs, TV shows, newspapers, and the like:

The *Washington Post* ran an interesting review of Frost's *Collected Poems*; its opinions about "Mending Wall" were especially interesting.

Geographical regions, but not compass directions:

Many movies are set in the West.

The Northern Hemisphere is the part of the earth that lies north of the equator.

The cultural division between East and West has persisted throughout modern times.

Titles of persons, if they appear immediately before the person's name:

President Barack Obama held a press conference last week.

Barack Obama, president of the United States, visited our town twice during his first term.

Political parties and philosophy, but not systems of government or individual adherents to a political philosophy:

The problems within the Communist Party foreshadowed the difficulties that communism would have in establishing itself.

The Republicans and Democrats often argue about how best to spread democracy to other countries.

WORD CHOICE (Standard 9)

Usage

Consider this sentence: The high school *principal* resigned for two *principal* reasons. If you think that the second *principal* is the wrong word (that it should be *principle*), think again. This usage is correct. You may be asked about words that are commonly confused and misused, as well as the use of words based on their grammatical appropriateness in a sentence, such as the distinction between *principal* and *principle*, *fewer* and *less*, and *lie* and *lay*. Here are some commonly confused pairs:

> *principal*—as an adjective, most important; as a noun, the chief authority.

> *principle*—always a noun: a fundamental law.

>> "We hold these principles to be self-evident."

> *affect*—usually a verb, meaning to *influence*; sometimes a noun, with a specific meaning in psychology.

>> "Her performance was adversely affected by the heat."

> *effect*—usually a noun, meaning something that results from something else; occasionally a verb, meaning *to cause to come into being*.

>> "The heat had no effect on his performance."

>> "Her persistence helped to effect the new zoning ordinance."

Connotative and Denotative Meanings

The denotative meaning of a word is its *literal,* dictionary definition: what the word denotes, or "means." The connotative meaning of a word is what the word connotes or "suggests"; it is a meaning apart from what the word literally means.

A writer should choose a word based on the tone and context of the sentence; this ensures that a word bears the appropriate connotation while still conveying some exactness in denotation. For example, a gift might be described as "cheap," but the directness of the word has a negative connotation—something cheap is something of little or no value. The word *inexpensive* has a more positive connotation, although *cheap* is a synonym for *inexpensive*." You may very well have to make a decision regarding the appropriateness of words and phrases within the context of a sentence.

Wordiness and Conciseness

Some questions will test your ability to detect redundancies (unnecessary repetitions), circumlocution (failure to get to the point), and padding with loose synonyms. These questions require you to select sentences that use as few words as possible to convey a message clearly, economically, and effectively.

Effective writing is concise. Wordiness, on the other hand, decreases the clarity of expression by cluttering sentences with unnecessary words. Of course, not all short sentences are better than long ones simply because they are brief. As long as a word serves a function, it should remain in the sentence. However, repetition of words, sounds, and phrases should be used only for emphasis or other stylistic reasons. Editing your writing will make a difference in its impact. Notice what revision does here:

UNREVISED: The medical exam that he gave me was entirely complete.

REVISED: The medical exam he gave me was complete.

UNREVISED: Larry asked his friend John, who was a good, old friend, if he would join him and go along with him to see the foreign film made in Japan.

REVISED: Larry asked his good, old friend John if he would join him in seeing the Japanese film.

UNREVISED: I was absolutely, totally happy with the present that my parents gave to me at 7 AM on the morning of my birthday.

REVISED: I was happy with the present my parents gave me on the morning of my birthday.

UNREVISED: It seems perfectly clear to me that although he went and got permission from the professor, he still should not have played that awful, terrible joke on the dean.

REVISED: It seems clear that, although he got permission from the professor, he should not have played that terrible joke on the dean.

TRANSITIONS AND COHERENCE (Standards 10 & 11)

On the Language Arts portion of the Test of Academic Proficiency, you will be asked to tell whether a particular passage develops its ideas well. You will also be asked to supply missing words, phrases, or sentences that would make a particular passage develop more logically. Let's look at the following passage, which is adapted from a similar passage that appeared in Chapter 2.

Passage

[1]That the area of obscenity and pornography is a difficult one for the Supreme Court is well documented. [2]The Court's numerous attempts to define obscenity have proven unworkable and left the decision to the subjective preferences of the justices. [3]Perhaps Justice Stewart put it best when, after refusing to define obscenity, he declared, but "I know it when I see it." [4]Does the Court literally have to see it to know it? [5]Specifically, what role does the fact-pattern, including the materials' medium, play in the Court's decision?

[6]Several recent studies employ fact-pattern analysis in modeling the Court's decision making. [7]These studies examine the fact-pattern or case characteristics, often with ideological and attitudinal factors, as a determinant of the decision reached by the Court. [8]In broad terms, these studies owe their theoretical underpinnings to attitude theory. [9]As the name suggests, attitude theory views the Court's attitudes as an explanation of its decisions.

[10]These attitudes, however, do not operate in a vacuum. [11]As Spaeth explains, "[t]he activation of an attitude involves both an object and the situation in which that object is encountered." [12]The objects to which the Court directs its attitudes are litigants. [13]The situation—the subject matter of the case—can be defined in broad or narrow terms. [14]One may define the situation as an entire area of the law (e.g., civil liberties issues). [15]On an even broader scale, the situation may be defined as the decision to grant certiorari or whether to defect from a minimum-winning coalition.

[16]Defining the situation with such broad strokes, _____, does not allow one to control for case content. [17]In many specific issue areas, the cases present strikingly similar patterns. [18]In examining the Court's search and seizure decisions, Segal found that a relatively small number of situational and case characteristic variables explain a high proportion of the Court's decisions.

[19]Despite Segal's success, efforts to verify the applicability of fact-pattern analysis in other issue areas and using broad-based factors have been slow in forthcoming. [20]Renewed interest in obscenity and pornography by federal and state governments as a result of lobbying campaigns by fundamentalist groups, the academic community, and other antipornography interest groups pro and con indicate the Court's decisions in this area <u>will get</u> closer examination.

[21]The Court's obscenity and pornography decisions _____ present an opportunity to study the Court's behavior in an area where the Court has granted significant decision-making authority to the states. [22]In *Miller v. California* (1973) the Court announced the importance of local community standards in obscenity determinations. [23]The Court's _____ behavior may suggest how the Court will react in other areas where it has chosen to defer to the states (e.g., abortion).

Questions

[*Note:* The superscript numbers that appear before the sentences in the passage are referred to as "Part" in the questions.]

1. This passage would be most appropriate in which type of publication?

    A. A popular newsmagazine such as *Time* or *The Atlantic*

    B. An editorial about pornography in a newspaper

    C. A chapter on pornography in a sociology textbook

    D. An article in a law journal

2. Which of the following phrases, if inserted in the blank in Part 16, would best help the reader understand the author's progression of ideas.

    A. consequently

    B. however

    C. nevertheless

    D. furthermore

3. In the final paragraph, which words or phrases, if inserted in order in the blanks, help the reader understand the author's logical sequence?

    A. in fact; foolish

    B. will; later

    C. also; subsequent

    D. theoretically; firm

4. Which of the following best describes the method of organization used by the author of this passage?

    A. problem and solution

    B. chronological order

    C. order of importance

    D. comparison and contrast

5. Which of the following sentences, if added between Parts 10 and 11, would be most consistent with the writer's purpose and intended audience?

    A. Situations with which the Court is faced are often quite complex.

    B. Supreme Court justices have been known to read newspapers as well as law journals.

    C. Pornography has been a point of public dispute for many decades now.

    D. If they did operate in a vacuum, predicting a justice's vote on a particular issue from his record before his appointment would be somewhat straightforward.

6. Which word would best replace the underlined words in Part 20?

    A. deserve

    B. are garnering

    C. will continue to elude

    D. have avoided

Answers

Keep in mind that the first step to answering these types of questions involves applying the Four-Step Approach discussed in Chapter 2. You cannot answer questions about the purpose, audience, or organization of a passage without first having analyzed it through the four-step approach. You will see that, in the practice test in this book and in the actual examination, passages are generally shorter than this passage; this one has been included so that you can review the Four-Step Approach while answering these questions.

The answer to Question 1 is **(D)**. The quotes from scholars eliminate (A) and (B) from consideration, because newspapers and magazines for general readers do not usually quote experts without identifying why they are worthy of being experts. Choice (B) is further eliminated by the fact that the passage takes no position that the average newspaper reader might act upon. The tone of the passage might conceivably be appropriate to choice (C), but the passage focuses on law rather than pornography.

The correct answer to Question 2 is **(B)**. The previous paragraph ended with a statement about a "broad scale," and the new paragraph begins by saying that looking at the broad scale is inadequate. This sentence, then, must convey that contrast, so choices (A) and (D) are immediately eliminated. Choice (C) conveys the correct general meaning, but the use of *nevertheless* directly before a negative—*does not*—would be confusing to a reader.

The correct answer to Question 3 is **(C)**. To find this answer, you will first have to notice that the author is switching topics from obscenity to states' rights; therefore, the choice (A) is eliminated, because *in fact* is a transition that signals an example of what has just been discussed. (In addition, nothing in the passage indicates that the author regards the Court's behavior as "foolish.") Choice (B) is wrong simply because the word *will* is not accurate: the decisions already do present an opportunity for further analysis. Choice (D)'s *theoretically* is plausible, but *firm* is definitely wrong because it does not describe the author's opinion of the Court's 1973 decision, which just announces the importance of local standards rather than making firm law regarding them.

Question 4's answer is **(D)**. Although a problem and solution are implied in the passage, there is no direct statement of the problem followed by a solution. Chronological order and order of importance are clearly not present here, but the writer does compare and contrast analytical methods and attempts to explicate their strengths and weaknesses.

The best answer to Question 5 is **(D)**. Choices (A) and (C) are far from the point of the paragraph, which concerns how justices reach decisions. The choice of (D) over (B) depends on the tone of the two sentences as well as the specific content. The content of the two sentences is similar, although the content of (D) is somewhat more on message. The tone of choice (B), however, is a bit flippant and would undoubtedly be out of place in most articles aimed at law scholars.

The best answer to Question 6 is **(A)**. Choice (D) contradicts the facts as presented in the paragraph, and choice (C) is out of line with the entire passage, which does give close examination to the subject. Choice (B) is technically correct (although not very informative for a final thought in a paragraph), but the word *garner* would be more at home in a newspaper article ("Duncan Garners Another Award") than in an article like this one.

SENTENCE AND PARAGRAPH STRUCTURE (Standard 12)

Parallelism

Sentences should use the same kind of grammatical construction for all items in a series—those usually joined by a coordinating conjunction (*and*, *but*, or, and *nor*). "No smoking, eating, or drinking" is parallel; "No smoking, food, or drinking" is not because *food* is not a verb form. Making elements parallel also requires knowledge of parallel correlative pairs, that is, the use of appropriate pairs together: *neither* and *nor*, *either* and *or*, *both* with *and*, *whether* with *or*, and *not only* with *but also*.

Parallel structure is used to express matching ideas. It refers to the grammatical balance of a series of any of the following:

Phrases. The squirrel ran *along the fence*, *up the tree*, and *into his hole* with a mouthful of acorns.

Adjectives. The job market is flooded with *very talented*, *highly motivated*, and *well-educated* young people.

Nouns. You will need a *notebook*, *pencil*, and *dictionary* for the test.

Clauses. The children were told to decide *which toy they would keep* and *which toy they would give away*.

Verbs. The farmer *plowed*, *planted*, and *harvested* his corn in record time.

Verbals. *Reading*, *writing*, and *calculating* are fundamental skills we should all possess.

Correlative Conjunctions. *Either* you will do your homework *or* you will fail. *Note:* Correlative conjunctions must be used as pairs and not mixed with other conjunctions, such as *neither* with *or* or *not only* with *also*.

Near-parallelisms. Sometimes a string of seemingly parallel thoughts are not in fact parallel. Consider this sentence: "I *have quit* my job, *enrolled* in school, and *am looking* for a reliable babysitter." In this sentence the writer has already *quit* and *enrolled* but is still looking for a babysitter; therefore she cannot include all three in a parallel structure. A good revision of this sentence is, "I have quit my job and enrolled in school, and I am looking for a babysitter."

Misplaced and Dangling Modifiers

As the name suggests, a misplaced modifier is one that is in the wrong place in the sentence. Misplaced modifiers come in all forms—words, phrases, and clauses. Sentences containing misplaced modifiers are often very comical: *Mom made me eat the spinach instead of my brother*. Misplaced modifiers, like the one in this sentence, are usually too far away from the word or words they modify. This sentence should read *Mom made me, instead of my brother, eat the spinach*.

Such modifiers as *only, nearly,* and *almost* should be placed next to the word they modify and not in front of some other word, especially a verb, that they are not intended to modify. For example, *I only sang for one reason* is wrong if the writer means to say that there was only one reason for singing.

A modifier is misplaced if it appears to modify the wrong part of the sentence or if the reader cannot be certain what part of the sentence the writer intended it to modify. To correct a misplaced modifier, move the modifier next to the word it describes.

UNREVISED: She served hamburgers to the men on paper plates.

REVISED: She served hamburgers on paper plates to the men.

A squinting modifier is one that may refer to either a preceding or a following word, leaving the reader uncertain about what it is intended to modify. Correct a squinting modifier by moving it next to the word it is intended to modify.

UNREVISED: Snipers who fired on the soldiers often escaped capture.

REVISED: Snipers who often fired on the soldiers escaped capture. OR Snipers who fired on the soldiers escaped capture often.

A dangling modifier is a modifier or verb in search of a subject: the modifying phrase (usually a participle phrase—an *-ing* word group or an *-ed* or an *-en* word group—or an infinitive phrase—a to + verb word group) has nothing to modify. It is figuratively *dangling* at the beginning or the end of a sentence. The sentences often look and sound correct at first glance: *To be a student government officer, your grades must be above average.* However, the verbal modifier has nothing to describe. You are supposed *to be a student government officer*; *your grades* cannot become an officer.

To correct a dangling modifier, reword the sentence by either (1) changing the modifying phrase to a clause with a subject, or (2) changing the subject of the sentence to the word that should be modified. Here are some other examples of correct revision of dangling modifiers:

UNREVISED: Shortly after leaving home, the accident occurred.

REVISED: Shortly after we left home, the accident occurred.

UNREVISED: To get up on time, a great effort was needed.

REVISED: To get up on time, I made a great effort.

Sentence Fragments

A fragment is an incomplete construction that either (1) lacks a subject or a verb or (2) is preceded by a subordinating conjunction (e.g., *because*, *which*, *when*, *although*). A complete construction, such as a sentence or an independent clause, expresses a complete thought.

UNREVISED: Traffic was stalled for ten miles on the freeway. Because repairs were being made on potholes. (The second "sentence" is a dependent, or subordinate, clause.)

REVISED: Traffic was stalled for ten miles on the freeway because repairs were being made on potholes.

UNREVISED: It was a funny story. One that I had never heard before. (The second "sentence" has no verb for its subject, "One.")

REVISED: It was a funny story, one that I had never heard.

Run-On/Fused Sentences

A run-on, or fused, sentence is not necessarily a long sentence or a sentence that the reader considers too long; in fact, a run-on might consist of two short sentences: *Dry ice does not melt it evaporates*. A run-on results when the writer fuses, or runs together, two separate sentences without any correct mark of punctuation separating them.

UNREVISED: Knowing how to use a dictionary is no problem each dictionary has a section in the front of the book that tells you how.

REVISED: Knowing how to use a dictionary is no problem. Each dictionary has a section in the front of the book that tells you how.

The most common type of run-on sentence is characterized by a comma splice—the incorrect use of only a comma to separate what are really two separate sentences. There are three quick ways to fix a comma splice: (1) replace the comma with a period and start a new sentence; (2) replace the comma with a semicolon; and (3) add a coordinating conjunction, such as *and* or *but*, after the comma.

UNREVISED: Bob bought dress shoes, a suit, and a nice shirt, he needed them for his sister's wedding.

REVISED: Bob bought dress shoes, a suit, and a nice shirt. He needed them for his sister's wedding.

UNREVISED: One common error in writing is incorrect spelling, the other is the occasional use of faulty diction.

REVISED: One common error in writing is incorrect spelling; the other is the occasional use of faulty diction.

UNREVISED: We have never won the track championship, we have won the cross-country title.

REVISED: We have never won the track championship, but we have won the cross-country title.

If one of the complete thoughts is subordinate to the other, you may also use a subordinate conjunction to connect the two:

UNREVISED: Neal won the award, he had the highest score.

REVISED: Neal won the award because he had the highest score.

Subordination, Coordination, and Predication

Suppose that you wanted to combine the information in these two sentences to create one statement: *I studied a foreign language. I found English quite easy.* How you decide to combine this information should be determined by the relationship you'd like to show between the two facts. *I studied a foreign language,* and *I found English quite easy* adds little or nothing to the original meaning. The **coordination** of the two ideas (connecting them with the coordinating conjunction *and*) is therefore ineffective. Using **subordination** instead (connecting the sentences with a subordinating conjunction) clearly shows the relationship between the expressed ideas:

After I studied a foreign language, I found English quite easy. OR

Because I studied a foreign language, I found English quite easy.

When using any conjunction—coordinating or subordinating—be sure that the sentence parts you are joining are in agreement:

> **UNREVISED:** She loved him dearly but not his dog.
>
> **REVISED:** She loved him dearly, but she did not love his dog. OR She loved him, but not his dog, dearly.

Another common mistake is to forget that each member of the pair must be followed by the same kind of construction.

> **UNREVISED:** She complimented her friends both for their bravery and thanked them for their kindness.
>
> **REVISED:** She both complimented her friends for their bravery and thanked them for their kindness.

While refers to time and should not be used as a substitute for *though*, *and*, or *but*.

> **UNREVISED:** While I'm usually interested in Fellini movies, I'd rather not go tonight.
>
> **REVISED:** Although I'm usually interested in Fellini movies, I'd rather not go tonight.

Where refers to a place and should not be used as a substitute for *that*.

> **UNREVISED:** We read in the paper where they are making strides in DNA research.
>
> **REVISED:** We read in the paper that they are making great strides in DNA research.

After words such as *reason* and *explanation*, use *that*, not *because*.

> **UNREVISED:** His explanation for his tardiness was because his alarm did not go off.
>
> **REVISED:** His explanation for his tardiness was that his alarm did not go off.

CHAPTER 4

Writing

This chapter was developed to help prepare you for taking the writing section of the Test of Academic Proficiency. In this chapter, you will find a list of the covered standards and an overview of basic writing strategies. By studying this chapter, you will be more aware of the broad range of objectives that are covered in the Test of Academic Proficiency Standard 13.

You will be guided through a step-by-step process of how to write an essay, from writing strategies to budgeting time during the exam. Even if you feel that you are a good writer, you should still study this chapter, because it will help you become familiar with essay writing. The strategies included are provided to help you write an essay that is to the point, easily understood, properly structured, well supported, and correct according to the rules of grammar. You will not be expected to write a best-selling book in order to pass this test, however, the more you practice the strategies provided in this review, the easier it will be for you to write a good essay.

Standard 13 **Prepare an organized, developed composition in edited English as used in the United States in response to instructions regarding content, purpose, and audience.**

The following are examples of content that may be covered under this standard.

13.1   Compose a unified, focused, and sustained piece of writing on a given topic using language and style appropriate to a specified audience, purpose, and occasion.

13.2 Take a position on a contemporary social or political issue and defend that position with reasoned arguments and supporting examples.

13.3 Use effective sentence structure and apply the standards of edited English in the United States.

13.4 Demonstrate the ability to spell, capitalize, and punctuate according to the standards of edited English in the United States.

The Test of Academic Proficiency contains a writing assignment that asks you to compose a composition, or written response, on a given subject. You will be evaluated on your ability to communicate the written message to a specified audience. The compositions are graded on the following criteria:

Focus (the clarity of the main idea);

Support/elaboration (supporting details are specific and clearly understood);

Organization (logical sequence of thoughts and ideas, and overall clarity of the work);

Grammar and conventions (the extent to which the response has no errors in usage, spelling, capitalization, punctuation, and the precision of word choice).

SCORING

The responses are graded on a scale from "6" to "1." Other possible scores are "U" (Unscorable) or "B"(Blank).

In an essay earning a high-range score (6 or 5), ideas are presented clearly, arguments are well organized, and there is extensive and specific supporting detail. The writer communicates through effective sentence structure and uses proper spelling, grammar, and punctuation.

In an essay scoring a mid-range score (4 or 3), ideas are well communicated, but supporting details might not be as precise or extensive as in a paper scoring 6. The ideas might be incomplete or generally ineffective. Minor errors in areas such as punctuation, spelling, word choice, or general usage are present.

A low-range score of 2 is given to essays that do not support the main idea with specific details, and in which the overall organization of the work is unclear. The purpose of the essay might need to be inferred because it is vaguely stated. Errors are found in word choice, usage, sentence structure, spelling, and punctuation.

The response score of 1 would be given to an essay that does not communicate the overall message and is lacking logical sequence of ideas. Often the main idea is not clearly stated, and supporting details are confusing. Common errors include incorrect use of language and sentence structure. Spelling and punctuation errors are found throughout the response.

A response given a U is deemed unscorable. A U score would be given if the essay is not on the given topic, is illegible, too short, or not written in English.

A response given a B is self-explanatory (i.e., a blank sheet that contains no answer).

Following the writing prompt in the practice test, examples are given for writing samples with a score of 1 or 2, 3 or 4, and 5 or 6. Included with each example is a discussion of what graders are looking for in relation to focus, support/elaboration, organization, and grammar and conventions.

GETTING STARTED

Carefully read the assignment before you begin to write. Think about your ideas and what you would like to communicate to the reader. You may wish to make an outline for the topic to help organize your thoughts, but be sure to write the final draft of your response in the test booklet. Your score will be based on what is written in the response booklet. When you have finished writing, be sure to review your work and make any changes you believe would enhance your score.

I. STRATEGIES FOR THE ESSAY

To give yourself the best chance of writing a good essay, you should follow these steps.

Before the test, this is your plan:

Step 1: Study the following review to enhance your ability to write an essay. Remember, the sharper your skills, the more likely you are to receive a passing grade on your writing sample.

Step 2: Practice writing an essay. The best way to do this is to complete the Practice Test.

Step 3: Learn and understand the directions so that you don't waste valuable time reading them on the test day. This will allow you to quickly review them before writing your essay.

Step 4: Develop your essay from the notes you have made. Present your position clearly and logically, making sure to provide adequate examples and/or support. Write your draft on scratch paper.

Step 5: Proofread your essay! Check every word for errors in spelling. Be sure that your sentences are concise and grammatically correct. Make any necessary revisions.

Step 6: Copy the final version of your essay into the response booklet.

Additional Tips

- Be sure that you have not strayed from your topic or introduced points that you have not explained.

- Vary your types of sentences so that your essay flows smoothly and is easy to read.

- Use vocabulary that suits your audience. Make sure not to insult your audience by using simple vocabulary, or by explaining things they already know. Likewise, do not alienate your audience by using complicated jargon, or by assuming that your readers are already familiar with the subject on which you are writing.

II. RECOGNIZING EFFECTIVE WRITING

Organization and Purposeful Development

For this test, you will need to recognize and generate the elements of an excellent essay. In essence, you will be taking the principles covered in this review and utilizing them to create your own original essay. With that in mind, read carefully the standards and explanations below to prepare you for what to look for in your own essay response.

Fast Facts

Use vocabulary that suits your audience.

Essay Writing

In academic writing, two purposes dominate essays:

1. Persuasion through argumentation using one, some, or all of the logical patterns described here.

2. Informing and educating through analysis and using one, some, or all of the logical patterns described here.

All of an essay's organizational strategies may be used to argue in writing. The author offers reasons and/or evidence so an audience will be inclined to believe the position that the author presents about the idea under discussion. Writers use seven basic strategies to organize information and ideas in essays to help prove their point (thesis). All of these strategies might be useful in arguing for an idea and persuading a reader to see the issue the writer's way. Your job is to use strategies that are appropriate to demonstrate your thesis. For example, you may wish to use comparison and contrast to demonstrate that one thing or idea is better or worse than another.

The following seven steps can be used to prove a thesis.

Seven Steps to Prove a Thesis

1. Show how a *process* or procedure does or should work, step by step, in time.

2. *Compare or contrast* two or more things or ideas to show important differences or similarities.

3. *Identify a problem* and then explain how to solve it.

4. *Analyze* into its components, or *classify* by its types or categories an idea or thing to show how it is put together, how it works, or how it is designed.

5. *Explain* why something happens to produce a particular result or set of results.

6. *Describe* the particular individual characteristics, beauty and features of a place, person(s), time, or idea.

7. *Define* what a thing is or what an idea means.

Depending upon the purpose of the essay, one pattern tends to dominate the discussion question. (For example, the writer might use description and explanation to define the varied meanings of "love.")

During this test you will be called upon to exercise control over your writing by using the writing process and by knowing the pitfalls of weak writing and correcting them. Using the steps outlined below, compose your essay in the order suggested and note the elements and qualities to correct during each stage of the process of composing your essay test response. Make any corrections you need during the appropriate stage of the writing process; to correct errors at the wrong stage may waste time and interfere with your producing the best essay response.

Composing Your Essay: Using the Writing Process

Some people (erroneously) think that writers just sit down and churn out a wonderful essay or poem in one sitting in a flash of genius and inspiration. This is not true. Writers use the writing process from start to finish to help them to write a clear document. If you do not reflect on your composition in stages and make changes as you develop it, you will not see all the problems or errors in it. Don't try to write an essay just once and leave the room. Stay and look through it. Reflect upon it using the writing process.

The writing process has five steps:

1. Prewriting, or planning time;

2. The rough draft;

3. Organizing and revising the ideas (not the words or sentences themselves);

4. Polishing, or editing (making sure sentences themselves are sentences, that the words you use are the right words, and that the spelling and punctuation are correct); and

5. Proofreading, to make sure no mistakes are left.

Using this process does not mean that you have to write five drafts. Write one draft (stages 1 and 2), leaving space for corrections (e.g., writing on every other line or on one side of a page only) and then working on the existing draft through the rest of the stages (3 through 5). If time allows, you may want to do the whole process on scrap paper and then copy the finished product onto the allotted test paper. But if you do copy it, make sure you proofread your copy to see whether, while transcribing it, you left anything out or said a word twice or made any other errors.

III. WRITING YOUR ESSAY

Prewriting/Planning Time

Read the essay question and decide on your purpose. Do you want to persuade your reader? Would you rather explain something?

> **SAMPLE:** "Television is bad for people."

Do you agree or disagree with this statement? Decide. Take a stand. Don't be non-committal. Write down the statement of your position.

> **SAMPLE:** "I agree that television is bad for people."
>
> or
>
> "Television is an excellent learning tool and is good for most people."

This is your thesis.

Consider Your Audience

The writer's responsibility is to write clearly, honestly, and cleanly for the reader's sake. Essays would be pointless without an audience. Why write an essay if no one wants or needs to read it? Why add evidence, organize your ideas, or correct bad grammar? The reason to do any of these things is that someone out there needs to understand what you mean to say. What would the audience need to know in order to believe you or to come over to your position? Imagine someone you know (visualize her or him) listening to you declare your position or opinion and then saying, "Oh yeah? Prove it!"

In writing your essay, make sure to answer the following questions: What evidence do you need to prove your idea to this skeptic? What would she disagree with you about? What does she share with you as common knowledge? What does she need to be told by you?

Control Your Point of View

We may write essays from one of three points of view, depending upon the essay's audience. The points of view below are discussed from informal to formal.

1. Subjective/Personal Point of View:

    "I think/believe/feel cars are more trouble than they are worth."

2. Second-Person Point of View:

    "If you own a car, you soon find out that it is more trouble than it is worth."

3. Third-Person Point of View (focuses on the idea, not what "I" think of it):

    "Cars are more trouble than they are worth."

For now, stick with one or another; don't switch your "point of view" in the middle. Any point of view that's properly supported is acceptable.

Consider Your Support

Next, during prewriting, jot down a few phrases that show ideas and examples that support your point of view. Do this quickly on a separate piece of paper for about five minutes. Don't try to outline—simply list things that you think might be important to discuss. After you have listed several, pick at least three to five things you want or need to discuss, and number them in the order of importance that is relevant to proving your point.

Write Your Rough Draft

Spend about ten to twenty minutes writing your rough draft. Looking over your pre-writing list, write down what you think is useful to prove your point in the order you think best to convince the reader. Be sure to use real evidence from your life experience or knowledge to support what you say. You do not have to draw evidence from books; your own life is equally appropriate.

For example, don't write, "Cars are more trouble to fix than bicycles," and then fail to show evidence for your idea. Give examples of what you mean: "For example, my father's Buick needs 200 parts to make one brake work, but my bicycle only has four pieces that make up the brakes, and I can replace those myself." Write naturally and quickly. Don't worry too much at this point about paragraphing, spelling, or punctuation—just write down what you think or want to say in the order determined on your list.

> **Fast Facts**
>
> The writer's responsibility is to write clearly, honestly, and cleanly for the reader's sake.

Transitions

To help the reader follow the flow of your ideas and to help unify the essay, use transitions to show the connections among your ideas. You may use transitions at the beginnings of paragraphs, or you may use them to show the connections among ideas within a single paragraph.

Here are some typical transitional words and phrases that you should use when writing your essay.

To link similar ideas, use the words:

again	equally important	in addition	of course
also	for example	in like manner	similarly
and	for instance	likewise	too
another	further	moreover	
besides	furthermore	or	

To link dissimilar or contradictory ideas, use words such as:

although	and yet	as if	but
conversely	even if	however	in spite of
instead	nevertheless	on the contrary	on the other hand
otherwise	provided that	still	yet

To indicate cause, purpose, or result, use:

as	consequently	hence	then
as a result	for	since	therefore
because	for this reason	so	thus

To indicate time or position, use words like:

above	at the present time	first	second
across	before	here	thereafter
afterward	beyond	meanwhile	thereupon
around	eventually	next	
at once	finally	presently	

To indicate an example or summary, use phrases such as:

as a result	in any case	in conclusion	in short
as I have said	in any event	in fact	on the whole
for example	in brief	in other words	to sum up
for instance			

Providing Evidence in Your Essay

You may employ any one of the seven steps previously listed to prove any thesis that you maintain is true. You may also call on evidence from one or all of the four following kinds of evidence to support the thesis of your essay. Identify which kind(s) of evidence you can use to prove the points of your essay. In test situations, most essayists use anecdotal evidence or analogy to explain, describe, or prove a thesis. But if you know salient facts or statistics, don't hesitate to call upon them.

1. Hard data (facts, statistics, scientific evidence, research)—documented evidence that has been verified.

2. Anecdotal evidence—stories from the writer's own experience and knowledge that illustrate a particular point or idea.

3. Expert opinions—assertions or conclusions, usually by authorities, about the matter under discussion.

4. Analogies—show a resemblance between one phenomenon and another.

Organizing and Reviewing the Paragraphs

The unit of work for revising is the paragraph. After you have written what you wanted to say based on your prewriting list, spend about twenty minutes revising your draft by looking to see whether you need to indent for paragraphs anywhere. If you do, make a proofreader's mark to indicate to the reader that you think a paragraph should start here. Check to see whether you want to add anything that would make your point of view more convincing. Be sure to supply useful transitions to keep up the flow and maintain the focus of your ideas. If you don't have room on the paper, or if your new paragraph shows up out of order, add that paragraph and indicate with a number or some other mark where you want it to go. Check to make sure that you gave examples or illustrations for your statements. In the examples below, two paragraphs are offered: one without concrete evidence and one with evidence for its idea. Study each. Note the topic sentence (T) and how that sentence is or is not supported with evidence.

Paragraphing with No Evidence

Television is bad for people. Programs on television are often stupid and depict crimes that people later copy. Television takes time away from loved ones, and it often becomes addictive. So, television is bad for people because it is no good.

In this example, the author has not given any concrete evidence for any of the good ideas presented. He just declares them to be so. Any one of the sentences above might make a good opening sentence for a whole paragraph. Take the second sentence, for example:

Watching television takes time away from other things. For example, all those hours people spend sitting in front of the tube, they could be working on building a chair or fixing the roof. (*Second piece of evidence*) Maybe the laundry needs to be done, but because people watch television, they may end up not having time to do it. Then Monday comes around again and they have no socks to wear to work—all because they couldn't stand to miss that episode of "Everybody Loves Raymond." (*Third piece of evidence*) Someone could be writing a letter to a friend in Boston who hasn't been heard from or written to for months. (*Fourth piece of evidence*) Or maybe someone misses the opportunity to take in a beautiful day in the park because she had to see "General Hospital." They might repeat "General Hospital," but this beautiful day only comes around once.

Watching television definitely keeps people from getting things done.

The primary evidence the author uses here is that of probable illustrations taken from life experience that are largely anecdotal. Always supply evidence. Three examples or illustrations of your idea per paragraph is a useful number. Don't go on and on about a single point. You don't have time. In order for a typical test essay to be fully developed, it should have about five paragraphs. They ought to be organized in the following manner:

Introduction: A paragraph that shows your point of view (thesis) about an issue and introduces your position with three general ideas that support your thesis.

Development: Three middle paragraphs that prove your position from different angles, using evidence from real life and knowledge. Each supporting paragraph in the middle should in turn support each of the three ideas you started out with in the introductory or thesis paragraph.

Conclusion: The last paragraph, which sums up your position and adds one final reminder of what the issue was, perhaps points to a solution:

So, television takes away from the quality of life and is therefore bad for human beings. We should be watching the sun, the sky, the birds, and each other, not the "boob tube."

Write a paragraph using this sentence as your focus: "Television takes valuable time away from our loved ones."

Check for Logic

Make sure that you present your argument in a logical manner. If you have not, you may not have proven your point. Your conclusion must follow from a logical set of premises, such as:

- Either/Or—The writer assumes that only two opposing possibilities may be attained: "Either _____, or this _____."

- Oversimplification—The writer simplifies the subject: "The rich only want one thing."

- Begging the question—The writer assumes she has proven something (often counterintuitive) that may need to be proven to the reader: "The death penalty actually increases, rather than deters, violent crime."

- Ignoring the issue—The writer argues against the truth of an issue due to its conclusion: "John is a good boy and, therefore, did not rob the store."

- Arguing against a person, not an idea—The writer argues that somebody's idea has no merit because he is immoral or personally stupid: "Eric will fail school because he is not doing well in gym class."

- Non sequitur—The writer leaps to the wrong conclusion: "Jake is from Canada; he must play hockey."

- Drawing the wrong conclusion from a sequence—The author attributes the outcome to the wrong reasons: "Betty married at a young age to an older man and now has three children and is therefore a housewife."

Fast Facts

Be sure to supply useful transitions to keep up the flow and maintain the focus of your ideas.

IV. POLISHING AND EDITING YOUR ESSAY

If the unit of work for revising is the paragraph, the unit of work for editing is the sentence. Check your paper for mistakes in editing. To help you in this task, use the following checklist.

Polishing Checklist

- Are all of your sentences *really* sentences, or have you written some fragments or run-on sentences?

- Are you using vocabulary correctly?

- Have you used a word that seems colloquial or too informal?

- Did you leave out punctuation anywhere? Did you capitalize, or not capitalize, correctly? Did you check for commas, periods, and quotation marks?

Proofreading

In the last three to five minutes, read your paper word for word, first forward and then backward, reading from the end to the beginning. Doing so can help you find errors that you may have missed by having read forward only.

Mathematics

The mathematics portion of the TAP test requires you to apply your mathematic knowledge of basic operations involving integers, fractions, decimals, proportions, and ratios. You will also be required to apply mathematical reasoning skills to analyze patterns and solve problems that involve geometry, measurement, algebra, data analysis, and probability.

This review was developed to help prepare you for taking the mathematics section of the Test of Academic Proficiency. In this chapter, you will find a list of the covered standards and an overview of basic mathematics skills. By studying this review and questions in the practice test, you will be more aware of the broad range of objectives that are covered in the Test of Academic Proficiency Standards 14, 15, 16, 17 and 18.

Standard 14   Solve problems involving integers, fractions, decimals, and units of measurement.

The following are examples of content that may be covered under this standard.

14.1   Solve problems involving integers, fractions, and decimals, including percentages.

14.2   Solve problems involving ratios and proportions.

14.3 Solve problems involving units of measurement, including U.S. customary and metric measurements, and conversions, including scientific notation (e.g., 6.05×10^8).

14.4 Use estimation skills to solve problems.

Standard 15 **Apply mathematical reasoning skills to analyze patterns and solve problems.**

The following are examples of content that may be covered under this standard.

15.1 Draw conclusions using inductive reasoning.

15.2 Draw conclusions using deductive reasoning.

15.3 Identify errors in mathematical explanations.

Standard 16 **Solve problems involving algebra and geometry.**

The following are examples of content that may be covered under this standard.

16.1 Graph numbers or number relationships.

16.2 Find the value of the unknown in a given one-variable equation.

16.3 Express one variable in terms of a second variable in two-variable equations.

16.4 Solve problems involving lines and angles.

16.5 Solve problems involving two- and three-dimensional geometric figures (e.g., perimeter and area problems, volume and surface area problems).

Standard 17 **Understand concepts and procedures related to data analysis and statistics.**

The following are examples of content that may be covered under this standard.

17.1 Interpret information from tables, line graphs, bar graphs, histograms, pictographs, and pie charts.

17.2 Recognize appropriate representations of various data in graphic form (discrete and continuous).

17.3 Demonstrate an understanding of fundamental statistical concepts (e.g., mean, correlation, standard deviation).

17.4 Interpret graphic and nongraphic representations of frequency distributions, percentiles, central tendency, variability, and correlation.

17.5 Demonstrate knowledge of basic concepts of probability using a variety of representations (e.g., word problems, Venn diagrams, tree diagrams).

Standard 18 **Solve applied problems using a combination of mathematical skills (including word problems involving one and two variables).**

The following are examples of content that may be covered under this standard.

18.1 Apply combinations of mathematical skills to solve a series of related problems.

18.2 Identify an equation to solve word problems involving one and two variables.

18.3 Apply number concepts and geometric principles to solve practical problems.

18.4 Apply statistical principles to analyze patterns and trends in data.

PROBLEM SOLVING WITH COMPUTATIONS (Standard 14)

Fractions

Before adding, fractions need to have common denominators. Thus, to add $\frac{1}{2}$ and $\frac{2}{3}$, change both fractions to equivalent fractions. These new equivalent fractions will have the same value as $\frac{1}{2}$ and $\frac{2}{3}$ and will have common (same) denominators, but will look different from the original fractions. The lowest common denominator is 6, because both of the original denominators can be changed into 6; $\frac{1}{2}$ can be written as $\frac{3}{6}$, and $\frac{2}{3}$ can be written as $\frac{4}{6}$.

After changing the "appearance" of $\frac{1}{2} + \frac{2}{3}$ to $\frac{3}{6} + \frac{4}{6}$, we can then simply add the numerators together, giving $\frac{7}{6}$ or $1\frac{1}{6}$.

When adding mixed fractions (those made up of a whole number and a fraction), add the fractions first, then—separately—the whole numbers. If the fractions add up to more than 1, add 1 to the whole number sum. For example, if, after adding, we have 3 and $1\frac{3}{4}$, the final sum is $4\frac{3}{4}$.

The algorithm for subtracting fractions is generally the same as that for adding—common denominators are required. A problem, however, may be encountered when attempting to subtract mixed fractions such as $3\frac{2}{5}$ and $1\frac{4}{5}$. Note that $\frac{4}{5}$ can't be subtracted from $\frac{2}{5}$ (without involving negative numbers.) The solution is to rename $3\frac{2}{5}$ as $2\frac{7}{5}$. (This is accomplished by "borrowing" 1, or $\frac{5}{5}$, from the 3.) The new problem—still equivalent to the original—is $2\frac{7}{5}$ minus $1\frac{4}{5}$, or $1\frac{3}{5}$.

When multiplying fractions, multiply the numerators together and the denominators together, then simplify the resulting product. For instance, $\frac{2}{3} \times \frac{3}{4}$ equals $\frac{6}{12}$, or $\frac{1}{2}$. There is no need to use common denominators (as with fraction addition and subtraction.)

If the numbers to be multiplied are mixed fractions, first rewrite them as "improper" fractions, such as $\frac{14}{3}$, then use the procedure described earlier.

To divide fractions, invert the divisor (or the "second" number; the one "doing the dividing") and multiply instead. In the case of $\frac{1}{5}$ divided by $\frac{3}{8}$, change the original problem to the equivalent problem $\frac{1}{5} \times \frac{8}{3}$. Using the algorithm for multiplying fractions, we get $\frac{8}{15}$ as the quotient.

Decimals

Decimal notation provides a different way of representing fractions whose denominators are powers of 10. The fraction $\frac{13}{100}$, for instance, is written as 0.13, $\frac{1}{1000}$ as 0.001, and so forth.

To add or subtract decimal numbers, arrange them vertically, aligning decimal points, then add or subtract as one would whole numbers. (A whole number can be written as a decimal numeral by placing a decimal point to its right, with as many zeros added as needed. Thus, 7 becomes 7.0, or 7.00, etc.) The decimal point then "drops down" directly into the sum or difference; its position is not shifted.

Using the traditional algorithm for multiplying decimal numbers does not require aligning decimal points; the numbers to be multiplied can simply be arranged vertically, with right "justification." The numbers can then be multiplied as if they were whole numbers. The number of digits to the right of the decimal point in the product should equal the total number of digits to the right of the two factors. Here is an example:

$$
\begin{array}{r}
1.64 \\
\times\ \ 0.3 \\
\hline
=0.492
\end{array}
$$

One method for dividing decimal numbers is to use the traditional whole number division algorithm, placing the decimal point properly in the answer. The number of digits to the right of the decimal point in the divisor is how far the decimal point in the quotient (the answer) should be moved to the right, with the decimal point in the dividend as our starting position. Here is an example:

$$0.3 \overline{\smash{)}\,1.44} \quad 4.8$$

Note that careful placement of digits when writing both the problem and the quotient help ensure a correct answer.

Operations

The rules for performing operations on integers (whole numbers and their negative counterparts) and on fractions and decimal numbers where at least one is negative are generally the same as the rules for performing operations on non-negative numbers. The trick is to pay attention to the sign (the positive or negative value) of each answer. The rules for multiplication and division when at least one negative number is involved are the same: two positives or two negatives give a positive, whereas "mixing" a positive and a negative gives a negative ($-5 \times 3 = -15$, for instance). When adding or subtracting and at least one negative number is involved, it may be useful to think of the values as money, with "adding" being thought of as "gaining," "subtracting" being thought of as "losing," positive numbers being seen as "credits" and negative numbers, "debts." (Careful: Adding or "gaining" -8 is like losing 8.)

Sometimes, mathematical expressions indicate several operations. When simplifying such expressions, there is a universally agreed-upon order for "doing" each operation. First we compute any multiplication or division, left to right. Then, compute any addition or subtraction, also left to right. (If an expression contains any parentheses, all computation within the parentheses must be completed first.) Think "Please excuse my dear aunt Sally." Treat exponential expressions ("powers") as multiplication. Thus, the expression $3 + 7 \times 4 - 2$ equals 29. (Multiply 7 by 4 before doing the addition and subtraction.)

Exponential notation is a way to show repeated multiplication more simply. $2 \times 2 \times 2$, for instance, can be shown as 2^3, and is equal to 8. (Note: 2^3 does not mean 2×3.)

Scientific notation provides a method for showing any numbers using exponents (although it is most useful for very large and very small numbers). A number is in scientific notation when it is shown as a number between 1 and 10 times a power of 10. Thus, the number 75,000 in scientific notation is shown as 7.5×10^4.

When solving a proportion such as $\frac{1}{6} = \frac{x}{300}$, it is common to complete a cross-multiplication where you multiply 1×300 and $6 \times x$. After that you set the two quantities equal to each other, resulting in $300 = 6x$. From there you solve for x and the resulting answer is $x = 50$. An example of where you may need to solve this type of problem is:

> If the ratio of boys to girls in a school is 2 to 3, and there are a total of 450 students in the school, how many of them are girls?

You would set up the proportion of $\frac{3}{5} = \frac{x}{450}$. Since there is a total of 5 parts students (2 parts boys and 3 parts girls) and 3 of those parts are girls, your first ratio would be $\frac{3}{5}$. Your second ratio would represent the actual student body. Since the total number of students in the school is 450, it would be placed in the denominator where the total parts is in the corresponding ratio. The variable x would represent the number of girls, which is the number you are trying to find. By solving the proportion, you would determine that the number of girls is 270.

Another skill you may need to use is estimation. For example, given the following problem:

> Estimate the number of busses you need if each bus holds 62 people and there are 525 people going on the trip.

You can round 62 to 60 and then you know that 540 is 60×9. Then you can estimate that you need 9 busses to hold all of the people who need transportation.

Other common mathematical notation symbols include the following:

> $<$ means "less than"
>
> $>$ means "greater than"
>
> $\neq$ means "not equal to"

≤ means "less than or equal to"

≥ means "greater than or equal to"

APPLYING MATHEMATICAL SKILLS TO ANALYZE PATTERNS (Standard 15)

Reasoning Skills

When presented with math or logic problems, including geometry problems, deductive reasoning may be helpful. Deductive reasoning is reasoning from the general to the specific, and is supported by deductive logic. Here is an example of deductive reasoning:

All humans who have walked on the moon are males (a general proposition). Neil Armstrong walked on the moon, therefore he is a male (a specific proposition).

Note that conclusions reached via deductive reasoning are sound only if the original assumptions are actually true.

With inductive reasoning, a general rule is inferred from specific observations (which may be limited). Moving from the statement "All fish I have ever seen have fins" (specific but limited observations) to "All fish have fins" (a general proposition) is an example of inductive reasoning. Conclusions arrived at via inductive reasoning are not necessarily true.

An example of how logical reasoning can be used to solve a geometry problem is given hereafter. (In this case deductive reasoning is used to find the measure of ∠J.)

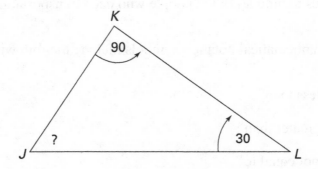

The sum of the measures of the three angles of any triangle is 180° (a general proposition). The sum of the measures of ∠K and ∠L is 120°; therefore, the measure of ∠J is 60° (a specific proposition).

Another example of using reasoning skills is given below:

If you place three square tables together, you will be able to seat 8 people around the tables (see diagram below). How many people would you be able to seat if you place 4 square tables together? 5 square tables? Etc.?

To solve this you would see a pattern emerge as you add each table. You would see that, for each additional table, you are adding two additional seats.

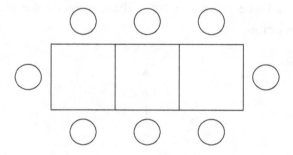

Therefore, you would be able to seat 10 people at four tables and 12 people at five tables.

At times, you will need to be able to recognize errors in mathematical reasoning. For example:

There are five toppings of pizza to choose from. How many two topping pizzas can you make?

You may think that you should multiply 5 × 4 (only four for the second choice) to find that there are 20 combinations of two-topping pizzas. You need to be able to recognize that the error in this reasoning is that a sausage/pepperoni pizza is the same as a pepperoni/sausage pizza. Therefore, you need to divide 20 by 2 to arrive at the correct answer of 10 unique two-topping pizzas.

SOLVING PROBLEMS INVOLVING ALGEBRA AND GEOMETRY (Standard 16)

Algebra

Two-Dimensional Graphing

The coordinate plane is useful for graphing individual ordered pairs and relationships. The coordinate plane is divided into four quadrants by an *x*-axis (horizontal) and a *y*-axis (vertical). The upper right quadrant is quadrant I, and the others (moving counterclockwise from quadrant I) are II, III, and IV.

Ordered pairs indicate the locations of points on the plane. For instance, (−3, 4) describes a point that is three units left from the center of the plane (the "origin") and four units up, as shown below.

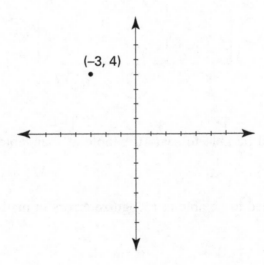

Sets of data can be paired to form many ordered pairs, which in turn can be graphed on the coordinate plane. Consider the following sets of data, which have been paired:

x	y
3	5
4	6
5	7
6	8

Considering each pairing individually, the following ordered pairs are produced: (3, 5), (4, 6), (5, 7), (6, 8). Plotting each pair on the coordinate plane produces the following graph:

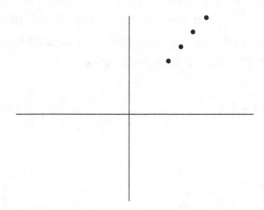

If the sets represent continuous change, the resulting graph may be a line (straight or curved in various ways). Often, relationships between sets of data can be shown as two variable equations or inequalities. Consider the following ordered pairs: (–4, –2), (–2, –1), (0, 0), (2, 1), (4, 2).

Note that the first value in each (the x value) is twice as big as the second (the y value). Assuming that the ordered pairs represent continuous change, the equation $x = 2y$ can be used to describe the relationship of the x values and the y values. It is helpful to think of the equation as stating that "x is always twice as big as y." We can show the equation on the coordinate plane by graphing at least two of the points, then connecting them, as shown below.

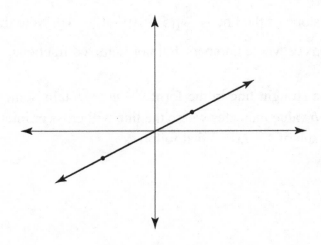

The generic equation $y = mx + b$ is a template for graphs on the plane that are straight lines. That form (sometimes called the "y-intercept form" of an equation) is especially useful because it tells two important characteristics of lines at a glance. The coefficient of x in the equation (or m) indicates the steepness, or slope of the line on the plane. The larger the absolute value of m, the steeper the slope of the line. (A number's absolute value is its distance from zero, giving no regard to negative signs.) Consider the two equations that follow and their accompanying graphs.

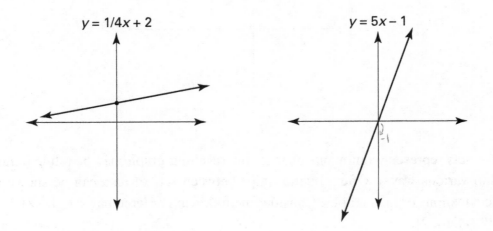

Note that the equation on the left has a small slope ($\frac{1}{4}$), so its graph is nearly horizontal. The other equation has a comparatively large slope (5), so it is steep.

If the coordinates of any two points of a straight line are known, the numerical slope of that line can easily be computed by finding the difference between the points' y values and dividing by the difference of the points' x values. For example, if (2, 5) and (4, 10) are points on a line, the slope of the line is $\frac{5}{2}$ [(5 − 10) ÷ (2 − 4)]. Note that slopes are generally shown as fractions or whole numbers, but not as mixed fractions.

The equation of a straight line in the form $y = mx + b$ tells something else about the line at a glance. The b value indicates where the line will cross or intercept the y (vertical) axis. Consider the graph of $y = 2x + 3$ that follows.

Note that the graph crosses the y-axis at a point that is 3 units above the origin. As long as the equation of a straight line is in the form $y = mx + b$, m gives the slope and b gives the y-intercept. (Note: If $b = 0$, the graph will pass through the origin. In that case, both the equation and the graph are referred to as direct variations.)

Other equations may produce curved graphs. For instance, $y = x^2$ produces the following graph, also known as a *parabola*.

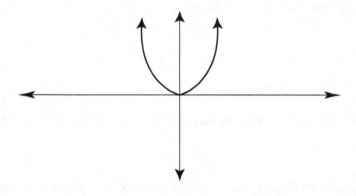

The equation $xy = 4$ is an inverse variation; it produces a graph known as a *hyperbola*, as shown below.

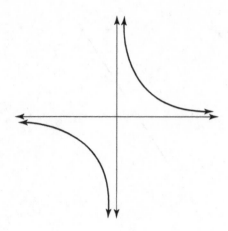

Solving One- and Two-Variable Equations

When attempting to solve one-variable equations, it is helpful to think of the task as that of producing a series of equivalent equations until, in the last equation, the variable has been isolated on one side. There are several ways to produce equivalent equations, but chiefly they are produced by performing identical operations on the two expressions making up the sides of equations. The equation $2x = 12$, for instance, can be solved by dividing both sides of the equation by 2, as follows:

$$\frac{2x}{2} = \frac{12}{2}$$

This then gives an equivalent equation of $x = 6$. Therefore, 6 is the solution to the original equation.

There are several caveats to observe when solving one-variable equations in this manner. One is that care must be taken to perform operations on entire expressions and not simply on "parts" of the expressions. In the example below, the last equation fails to give a solution to the original equation because, in the second step, only part of the expression $(2x + 8)$ has been divided by 2.

$$2x + 8 = 14$$

$$\frac{2x}{2} + 8 = \frac{14}{2}$$

$$x + 8 = 7$$

$$x = -1$$

(The correct answer is $x = 3$.)

Remember to avoid dividing by zero. That operation is considered meaningless and will not provide a solution. Also, not all single-variable equations have solutions. The equation $0x + 3 = 9$, for instance, has no real number solutions. If the variable carries an exponent, as in $x^2 = 16$, taking the square root of each side of the equation produces the solutions. (Note that both 4 and –4 work.)

"Solving one variable in terms of a second" simply means rewriting multivariable equations such that the desired variable is isolated on one side of the equation. For instance, the equation $x - 3y = 5$ can be rewritten as $x = 3y + 5$. The variable x has been solved in terms of the second variable y.

Solving a system of two-variable linear equations (such as $y = x + 6$ and $2y = 4x$) means finding the ordered pair (or pairs) of numbers that solves both equations simultaneously. Using trial and error, we can see that (6, 12) works in both of the equations above. There are also more formal methods for solving systems of two-variable equations. If we graph each equation on the coordinate plane, the point of intersection (if any) will give the solution to the system. Another method is to add or subtract one equation from the other, with the intention of eliminating one variable in the process, enabling us to solve for one variable, then the other. (One or both equations may first require multiplication in order to "line up" variables with opposite coefficients.) In the example that follows, the system of $y = x + 6$ and $2y = 4x$ has been solved using multiplication and addition.

$$y = x + 6$$

$$2y = 4x$$

$$-27 = -2x - 12$$

$$2y = 4x$$

$$0 = 2x - 12$$

$$x = 6$$

If $x = 6$, y must equal 12, so the solution to the system is (6, 12).

Geometry

The following are formulas for finding the areas of basic polygons (informally defined as closed, coplanar geometric figures with three or more straight sides). Abbreviations used are as follows:

A = area

l = length

w = width

h = height

b = length of the base

Triangle (a three-sided polygon): $A = \dfrac{b \times h}{2}$ (Note that, as shown in the figure that follows, the height of a triangle is not necessarily the same as the length of any of its sides.)

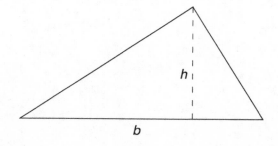

Rectangle (a four-sided polygon with four right angles): $A = l \times w$

Parallelogram (a four-sided polygon with two pairs of parallel sides): $A = l \times w$. (Note that, as with triangles, and as shown in the figure below, the height of a parallelogram is not necessarily the same as the length of its sides.)

The **area of a circle** can be found by squaring the length of its radius, then multiplying that product by π. The formula is given as $A = \dfrac{\pi r^2}{2}$. (π, or pi, is the ratio of a circle's circumference to its diameter. The value of π is the same for all circles; approximately 3.14159. The approximation 3.14 is adequate for many calculations.) The approximate area of the circle shown below can be found by squaring 6 (giving 36), then multiplying 36 by 3.14, giving an area of about 113 square units.

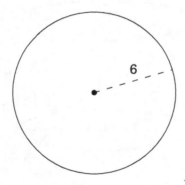

Volume

Here are several commonly used volume formulas:

The volume of a rectangular solid is equal to the product of its length, width, and height: $A = l \times w \times h$. (A rectangular solid can be thought of as a box, wherein all intersecting edges form right angles.)

A **prism** is a polyhedron with two congruent, parallel faces (called bases) and whose lateral (side) faces are parallelograms. The volume of a prism can be found by multiplying the area of the prism's base by its height. The volume of the triangular prism shown hereafter is 60 cubic units. (The area of the triangular base is 10 square units, and the height is 6 units.)

$V = A_{base} \times h$

A **cylinder** is like a prism in that it has parallel faces, but its rounded "side" is smooth. The formula for finding the volume of a cylinder is the same as the formula for finding the volume of a prism: The area of the cylinder's base is multiplied by the height. The volume of the cylinder in the following figure is approximately 628 cubic units ($5 \times 5 \times \pi \times 8$).

$V = A_{base} \times h$

$A_{base} = \dfrac{\pi r^2}{2} = \dfrac{5 \times 5 \times \pi}{2}$

$V = \dfrac{25\pi}{2} \times 8 = 100\pi$

$V \approx 314 \text{ cubic units}$

A property of all triangles is that the sum of the measures of the three angles is 180°. If, therefore, the measures of two angles are known, the third can be deduced using addition, then subtraction.

Right triangles (those with a right angle) have several special properties. A chief property is described by the Pythagorean Theorem, which states that in any right triangle with legs (shorter sides) a and b, and hypotenuse (the longest side) c, the sum of the squares of the sides will be equal to the square of the hypotenuse ($a^2 + b^2 = c^2$). Note that in the right triangle shown hereafter, $3^2 + 4^2 = 5^2$.

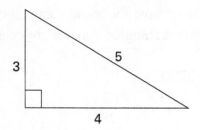

Applying Reasoning Skills

Geometric figures are *similar* if they have the exact same shapes, even if they do not have the same sizes. In transformational geometry, two figures are said to be similar *if and only if* a similarity transformation maps one figure onto the other. In the figure that follows, triangles *A* and *B* are similar.

Corresponding angles of similar figures have the same measure, and the lengths of corresponding sides are proportional. In the similar triangles below, $\angle A \cong \angle D$ (meaning "angle *A* is congruent to angle *D*"), $\angle B \cong \angle E$, and $\angle C \cong F$. The corresponding sides of the triangles below are proportional, meaning that:

$$\frac{AB}{DE} = \frac{BC}{EF} = \frac{CA}{FD}$$

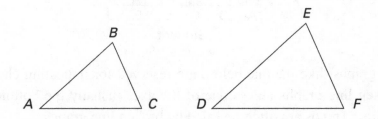

Figures are *congruent* if they have the same shape and size. (Congruent figures are also similar.) In the figure below, rectangles *A* and *B* are congruent.

Straight lines within the same plane that have no points in common (that is, they never cross) are parallel lines. Note that the term *parallel* is used to describe the relationship between two coplanar lines that do not intersect. Lines that are not coplanar—although they never cross—are not considered to be parallel. Coplanar lines crossing at right angles (90°) are perpendicular.

DATA ANALYSIS AND STATISTICS (Standard 17)

Interpreting Information from Graphs, Tables, or Charts

Graphs, tables and charts come in many different forms; most simply represent numerical data in neat visual formats. A bar graph, like the one below, typically shows "how much" for each of many categories (or persons, or time periods, or whatever).

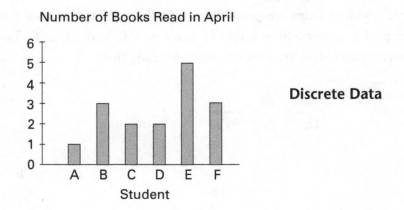

Broken line graphs, like the one below, are reserved for indicating change over time. Do not use broken line graphs unless one of the axes (usually the bottom or horizontal axis) indicates time. Trends are often revealed by broken line graphs.

Average monthly temperature,
January–June 1996, Chicago

Continuous Data

Pie graphs (also known as circle graphs or pie charts) often show how finite quantities are "split up." As with the example below, pie graphs may not necessarily be accompanied by specific numeric values. They are especially good for showing relative amounts or allotments at a glance.

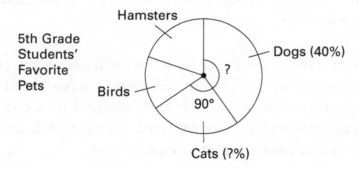

Because pie graphs are circles, the angle formed at the center by the boundaries of each category can be determined from the fact that the circle contains 360°. For example, if dogs are the favorite pets of 40% of fifth graders, what is the central angle? (**Answer:** $40\% \times 360° = .4 \times 360° = 144°$.) If the central angle of the "Cats" portion of the graph is 90°, what percentage of fifth graders prefer cats? (**Answer:** $90/360 = 1/4 = 25\%$.)

The graphs of functions can be shown on the coordinate plane. Such graphs always indicate a continuous (although not necessarily consistent) "movement" from left to right. Below left is the graph of a function; the graph on the right is not a function.

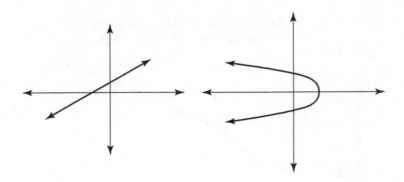

A key to interpretation of graphs, tables, and charts is to pay close attention to labels. Specific axes labels are also important. Don't assume anything about what a graph, table, or chart might be saying without carefully reading all labeled elements.

Statistical Concepts

The term *data* refers to numerical information acquired by counting or measuring. The number of students in a class, their test scores on the SAT, and their individual heights are all examples of data.

Data can be represented in *discrete* or *continuous* form, depending on what they represent. If data are discrete, there are gaps between them. The bar graph is a common way to depict discrete data. Discrete data are generally obtained from counting rather than measuring. Continuous data are usually represented by an unbroken line on a graph, and they are usually obtained by measuring rather than counting.

Here is a list of other statistical concepts that will be helpful to know for the test:

mean   The mean is the sum of a set of numbers divided by the quantity of numbers *n* in the set. It gives the *average* value of a data set.

range   The range is the measure of spread (*variation*) that is the difference between the largest value and the smallest value in a set of data.

sample survey   This is a survey of a population, usually human, made by taking a sample judged to be representative of the population. Use of a random mechanism for choosing the sample is essential for validity and believability.

spread of data   Spread, or **variation**, describes the degree to which data are spread out around their center. Useful measures of spread include the standard deviation and range.

standard deviation   This is the most commonly used expression of spread, or variation, of data. The higher the standard deviation, the higher is the degree of spread around the center of the data (that is, the data are more inconsistent with each other).

median   The median is the center value in a set of numbers: there are an equal number of values above and below it.

percentiles   These are the measures of where a piece of data stands in relation to the other data in its set. Perhaps best known from standardized tests, percentiles tell how many other data are lower in value. For instance, a test-taker might have a raw score of 82% (that is, 82% of the answers correct) but rank in the 91st percentile, meaning that 90% of all test-takers received lower raw scores. The median occurs at the 50th percentile.

frequency distributions   These represent the probability that a statistic of interest will fall in a certain interval; for example, the height of a person chosen at random may follow the normal distribution. Following are some samples of kinds of distributions, with location of the means and medians indicated:

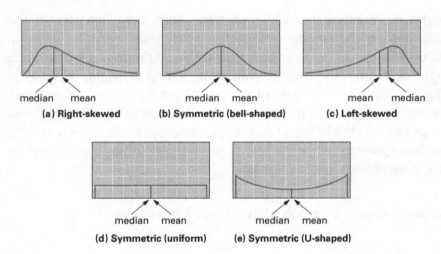

median   mean
(a) Right-skewed

median   mean
(b) Symmetric (bell-shaped)

mean   median
(c) Left-skewed

median   mean
(d) Symmetric (uniform)

median   mean
(e) Symmetric (U-shaped)

Symmetric (bell-shaped) distribution (shown in figure (b) above) is the famous normal, or bell-shaped, curve on which tests are often said to be graded. Notice that more scores fall in the middle here than on the high or low ends. In the right-skewed distribution, shown in figure (a) above, more of the scores are low, and in figure (c) above, more of the scores are high (assuming that all of these graphs represent test scores). The distribution in figure (d) shows that the scores (all scores) are distributed equally from high to low, and figure (e) shows a distribution in which most scores were either high or low, with very few being average. Notice that in figure (a), the right-skewed distribution, the mean is higher than the median, and in figure (c) the median is higher than the mean.

correlation Correlation is the relationship between two variables. For example, a graph of tar and nicotine in cigarettes might look like this:

Each dot represents a particular cigarette, and the placement of the dot depends on the amounts of its tar (x-axis) and nicotine (y-axis). Drawings like this are called scatterplots. You could draw a straight line through this scatterplot, and it would go up and to the right, because, in general, the higher the amount of tar, the higher the amount of nicotine. The amounts of tar and nicotine are thus positively correlated. Some variables are negatively correlated; for instance, the weight of a vehicle would be negatively correlated with gas mileage if several models of vehicle were plotted in a scatterplot.

Here are some other scatterplots with varying kinds of correlation:

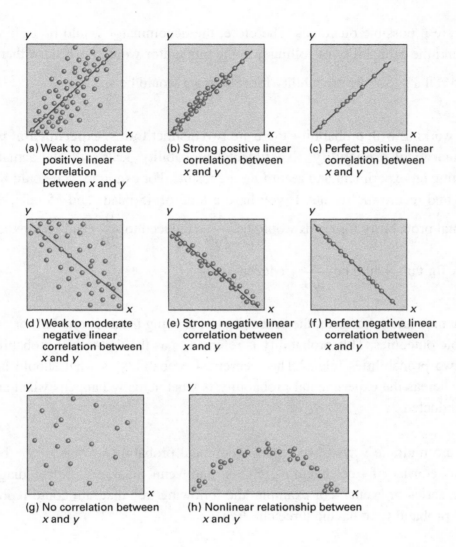

(a) Weak to moderate positive linear correlation between x and y

(b) Strong positive linear correlation between x and y

(c) Perfect positive linear correlation between x and y

(d) Weak to moderate negative linear correlation between x and y

(e) Strong negative linear correlation between x and y

(f) Perfect negative linear correlation between x and y

(g) No correlation between x and y

(h) Nonlinear relationship between x and y

When a correlation is linear or almost linear, you can use the graph to make predictions. For example, in the graph of tar and nicotine above, you could predict with a fair amount of certainty that a cigarette with 10 mg of tar would have between 0.7 and 0.8 mg of nicotine. In scatterplots without a linear correlation (graphs g and h above), it's much harder to predict what y would be given x; in fact, in graph (g), it's nearly impossible.

Probability

Probability is an indication of the likelihood of an event happening. It is usually written as a fraction where the numerator indicates the number of successful outcomes and the denominator indicates the total possible outcomes. For example, if you roll a single die, there are 6 possible outcomes. Therefore, the denominator would be 6. If you were asked to find the probability of rolling a 3, the numerator would be 1 since there is only one way to roll a 3. So, the probability for rolling a 3 would be $\frac{1}{6}$.

When working with probability, there are two distinct forms: **experimental probability** and **theoretical probability**. Experimental probability deals with the actual process of conducting an experiment and recording the results. For example, you could flip a coin 100 times and record the results. If you have a total of 45 heads and 55 tails, then your experimental probability for heads would be $\frac{45}{100}$ (reduced to $\frac{9}{20}$) and your experimental probability for tails would be $\frac{55}{100}$ (reduced to $\frac{11}{20}$).

As you may know, however, the probability of flipping heads is one-half or one out of two possible outcomes. This probability is referred to as the theoretical probability. How do these two probabilities relate? The theoretical probability is what should happen in "theory," whereas the experimental probability is what actually happens when an experiment is conducted.

There are multiple ways to represent theoretical probability. Some of the basic representations consist of tree diagrams, charts, and Venn diagrams. A tree diagram can represent a series of events. For example, the following tree diagram could represent the theoretical probability of having three children.

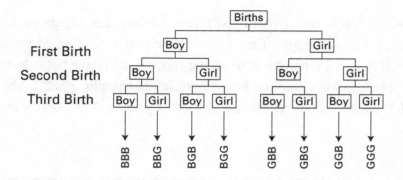

From this tree diagram you could answer several different questions. For example, what is the probability that you would have all children of the same sex? To answer this question you would see that there are two outcomes BBB and GGG where all three children would be of the same sex. This theoretical probability would be 2 out of 8 possible birth patterns. Therefore, the probability of having all same sex births would be $\frac{2}{8}$ which would be reduced to $\frac{1}{4}$.

Another representation you could use to show theoretical probability would be a chart. The following chart shows the outcomes of rolling two dice and then finding the sum of the dice.

	1	2	3	4	5	6
1	2	3	4	5	6	7
2	3	4	5	6	7	8
3	4	5	6	7	8	9
4	5	6	7	8	9	10
5	6	7	8	9	10	11
6	7	8	9	10	11	12

From this table you could state that the probability of rolling a sum of 7 is 6 out of 36 or $\frac{6}{36}$, which reduces to $\frac{1}{6}$.

One other representation that could be used is a Venn diagram. From the Venn diagram shown below, you could find the probability that a child likes only vanilla ice cream.

Favorite Flavors of Ice Cream

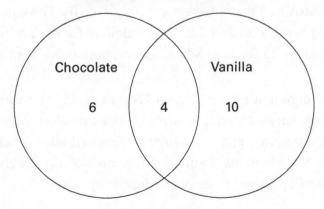

Chocolate   Vanilla

6   4   10

From this Venn diagram, you can tell that 10 out of 20 children like only vanilla ice cream. This probability would be 10 out of 20 or $\frac{10}{20}$, which reduces to $\frac{1}{2}$.

One other form of probability can be given in word format. Consider the following problem:

> A bag of marbles contains 3 red marbles, 2 yellow marbles, 7 green marbles, and 3 blue marbles. If you draw one marble, what is the probability that you will *not* draw a green marble?

Since there are 8 marbles that are not green, the probability of not drawing a green marble would be 8 out of 15 possible marbles, which gives us $\frac{8}{15}$ as our answer.

COMBINATION PROBLEMS (Standard 18)

Solving Word Problems Involving One and Two Variables

One helpful approach when attempting to solve algebraic word problems is to translate the word problem into an equation (or, sometimes, an inequality), then solve the equation. Consider the word problem:

> The Acme Taxicab Company charges riders 3 dollars just for getting into the cab, plus 2 dollars for every mile or fraction of a mile driven. What would be the fare for a 10-mile ride?

Translating the words into math, we get $x = 3 + (2 \times 10)$. The equation can be read as "the unknown fare (x) is equal to 3 dollars plus 2 dollars for each of the 10 miles driven." Solving the equation gives 23 for x, so $23 is the solution to the word problem.

There are several common translations to keep in mind: The word *is* often suggests an equals sign; *of* may suggest multiplication, as does *product*. *Sum* refers to addition; *difference* suggests subtraction; and a *quotient* is obtained after dividing. The key when translating words into math is to make sure that the equation accurately matches the information and the relationships given in the word problem.

When converting word problems into mathematical problems, the choice of operations is crucial to success. Often, individual words and phrases translate into numbers and operations symbols, and making sure that the translations are reasonable is important. Consider this word problem:

Roberto babysat for the Yagers one evening. They paid him $5 just for coming over to their house, plus $7 for every hour of sitting. How much was he paid if he babysat for 4 hours?

"Plus" indicates addition, and "for every hour" suggests multiplication. Thus, the computational work can be set up like this: 5 + (7 × 4) = Roberto's earnings. It would have been unreasonable to use a multiplication symbol in place of the addition sign. He earned $5 plus $7 for each of 4 hours.

Each word problem requires an individual approach, but keeping in mind the reasonableness of the computational setup should be helpful.

In the following problem you will need to use geometric reasoning and computational skills to solve a problem.

Below is a diagram of a backyard. In the center is a fountain that has a concrete walkway. Find the area of grass in the backyard.

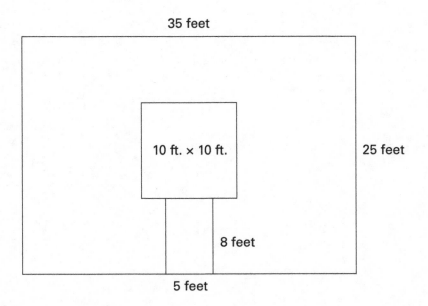

35 feet

10 ft. × 10 ft.

25 feet

8 feet

5 feet

Using the area formula, you could find that the total area of the backyard is 25 ft. × 35 ft., which is 875 square feet. The fountain is 10 ft. × 10 ft. or 100 square feet. The area of the walkway is 8 ft. × 5 ft. which is 40 square feet. If you add the 100 square feet for the fountain and the 40 square feet for the concrete walkway, you get the area of the backyard that is not grass. Subtract this 140 square feet from the total 875 square feet and you arrive at 735 square feet of grass.

PRACTICE TEST

ILTS Test of Academic Proficiency (400)

Also available at the REA Study Center (*www.rea.com/studycenter*)

This practice exam is also available at the REA Study Center (*www.rea.com/studycenter*). Since the ILTS Test of Academic Proficiency is offered only as a computer-based test, we recommend that you take the online version of this practice test to simulate the test-day experience and to receive these added benefits:

- **Timed testing conditions** – helps you gauge how much time you can spend on each question
- **Automatic scoring** – find out how you did on the test, instantly
- **On-screen detailed explanations of answers** – gives you the correct answer and explains why the other answer choices are wrong
- **Diagnostic score reports** – pinpoint where you're strongest and where you need to focus your study

ANSWER SHEET FOR PRACTICE TEST

1. (A) (B) (C) (D)
2. (A) (B) (C) (D)
3. (A) (B) (C) (D)
4. (A) (B) (C) (D)
5. (A) (B) (C) (D)
6. (A) (B) (C) (D)
7. (A) (B) (C) (D)
8. (A) (B) (C) (D)
9. (A) (B) (C) (D)
10. (A) (B) (C) (D)
11. (A) (B) (C) (D)
12. (A) (B) (C) (D)
13. (A) (B) (C) (D)
14. (A) (B) (C) (D)
15. (A) (B) (C) (D)
16. (A) (B) (C) (D)
17. (A) (B) (C) (D)
18. (A) (B) (C) (D)
19. (A) (B) (C) (D)
20. (A) (B) (C) (D)
21. (A) (B) (C) (D)
22. (A) (B) (C) (D)
23. (A) (B) (C) (D)
24. (A) (B) (C) (D)
25. (A) (B) (C) (D)
26. (A) (B) (C) (D)
27. (A) (B) (C) (D)
28. (A) (B) (C) (D)
29. (A) (B) (C) (D)
30. (A) (B) (C) (D)

31. (A) (B) (C) (D)
32. (A) (B) (C) (D)
33. (A) (B) (C) (D)
34. (A) (B) (C) (D)
35. (A) (B) (C) (D)
36. (A) (B) (C) (D)
37. (A) (B) (C) (D)
38. (A) (B) (C) (D)
39. (A) (B) (C) (D)
40. (A) (B) (C) (D)
41. (A) (B) (C) (D)
42. (A) (B) (C) (D)
43. (A) (B) (C) (D)
44. (A) (B) (C) (D)
45. (A) (B) (C) (D)
46. (A) (B) (C) (D)
47. (A) (B) (C) (D)
48. (A) (B) (C) (D)
49. (A) (B) (C) (D)
50. (A) (B) (C) (D)
51. (A) (B) (C) (D)
52. (A) (B) (C) (D)
53. (A) (B) (C) (D)
54. (A) (B) (C) (D)
55. (A) (B) (C) (D)
56. (A) (B) (C) (D)
57. (A) (B) (C) (D)
58. (A) (B) (C) (D)
59. (A) (B) (C) (D)
60. (A) (B) (C) (D)

61. (A) (B) (C) (D)
62. (A) (B) (C) (D)
63. (A) (B) (C) (D)
64. (A) (B) (C) (D)
65. (A) (B) (C) (D)
66. (A) (B) (C) (D)
67. (A) (B) (C) (D)
68. (A) (B) (C) (D)
69. (A) (B) (C) (D)
70. (A) (B) (C) (D)
71. (A) (B) (C) (D)
72. (A) (B) (C) (D)
73. (A) (B) (C) (D)
74. (A) (B) (C) (D)
75. (A) (B) (C) (D)
76. (A) (B) (C) (D)
77. (A) (B) (C) (D)
78. (A) (B) (C) (D)
79. (A) (B) (C) (D)
80. (A) (B) (C) (D)
81. (A) (B) (C) (D)
82. (A) (B) (C) (D)
83. (A) (B) (C) (D)
84. (A) (B) (C) (D)
85. (A) (B) (C) (D)
86. (A) (B) (C) (D)
87. (A) (B) (C) (D)
88. (A) (B) (C) (D)
89. (A) (B) (C) (D)
90. (A) (B) (C) (D)

91. Ⓐ Ⓑ Ⓒ Ⓓ
92. Ⓐ Ⓑ Ⓒ Ⓓ
93. Ⓐ Ⓑ Ⓒ Ⓓ
94. Ⓐ Ⓑ Ⓒ Ⓓ
95. Ⓐ Ⓑ Ⓒ Ⓓ
96. Ⓐ Ⓑ Ⓒ Ⓓ
97. Ⓐ Ⓑ Ⓒ Ⓓ
98. Ⓐ Ⓑ Ⓒ Ⓓ
99. Ⓐ Ⓑ Ⓒ Ⓓ
100. Ⓐ Ⓑ Ⓒ Ⓓ
101. Ⓐ Ⓑ Ⓒ Ⓓ
102. Ⓐ Ⓑ Ⓒ Ⓓ
103. Ⓐ Ⓑ Ⓒ Ⓓ
104. Ⓐ Ⓑ Ⓒ Ⓓ
105. Ⓐ Ⓑ Ⓒ Ⓓ
106. Ⓐ Ⓑ Ⓒ Ⓓ
107. Ⓐ Ⓑ Ⓒ Ⓓ
108. Ⓐ Ⓑ Ⓒ Ⓓ
109. Ⓐ Ⓑ Ⓒ Ⓓ
110. Ⓐ Ⓑ Ⓒ Ⓓ
111. Ⓐ Ⓑ Ⓒ Ⓓ
112. Ⓐ Ⓑ Ⓒ Ⓓ
113. Ⓐ Ⓑ Ⓒ Ⓓ
114. Ⓐ Ⓑ Ⓒ Ⓓ
115. Ⓐ Ⓑ Ⓒ Ⓓ
116. Ⓐ Ⓑ Ⓒ Ⓓ
117. Ⓐ Ⓑ Ⓒ Ⓓ

118. Ⓐ Ⓑ Ⓒ Ⓓ
119. Ⓐ Ⓑ Ⓒ Ⓓ
120. Ⓐ Ⓑ Ⓒ Ⓓ
121. Ⓐ Ⓑ Ⓒ Ⓓ
122. Ⓐ Ⓑ Ⓒ Ⓓ
123. Ⓐ Ⓑ Ⓒ Ⓓ
124. Ⓐ Ⓑ Ⓒ Ⓓ
125. Ⓐ Ⓑ Ⓒ Ⓓ
126. Ⓐ Ⓑ Ⓒ Ⓓ
127. Ⓐ Ⓑ Ⓒ Ⓓ
128. Ⓐ Ⓑ Ⓒ Ⓓ
129. Ⓐ Ⓑ Ⓒ Ⓓ
130. Ⓐ Ⓑ Ⓒ Ⓓ
131. Ⓐ Ⓑ Ⓒ Ⓓ
132. Ⓐ Ⓑ Ⓒ Ⓓ
133. Ⓐ Ⓑ Ⓒ Ⓓ
134. Ⓐ Ⓑ Ⓒ Ⓓ
135. Ⓐ Ⓑ Ⓒ Ⓓ
136. Ⓐ Ⓑ Ⓒ Ⓓ
137. Ⓐ Ⓑ Ⓒ Ⓓ
138. Ⓐ Ⓑ Ⓒ Ⓓ
139. Ⓐ Ⓑ Ⓒ Ⓓ
140. Ⓐ Ⓑ Ⓒ Ⓓ
141. Ⓐ Ⓑ Ⓒ Ⓓ
142. Ⓐ Ⓑ Ⓒ Ⓓ
143. Ⓐ Ⓑ Ⓒ Ⓓ
144. Ⓐ Ⓑ Ⓒ Ⓓ

145. Ⓐ Ⓑ Ⓒ Ⓓ
146. Ⓐ Ⓑ Ⓒ Ⓓ
147. Ⓐ Ⓑ Ⓒ Ⓓ
148. Ⓐ Ⓑ Ⓒ Ⓓ
149. Ⓐ Ⓑ Ⓒ Ⓓ
150. Ⓐ Ⓑ Ⓒ Ⓓ
151. Ⓐ Ⓑ Ⓒ Ⓓ
152. Ⓐ Ⓑ Ⓒ Ⓓ
153. Ⓐ Ⓑ Ⓒ Ⓓ
154. Ⓐ Ⓑ Ⓒ Ⓓ
155. Ⓐ Ⓑ Ⓒ Ⓓ
156. Ⓐ Ⓑ Ⓒ Ⓓ
157. Ⓐ Ⓑ Ⓒ Ⓓ
158. Ⓐ Ⓑ Ⓒ Ⓓ
159. Ⓐ Ⓑ Ⓒ Ⓓ
160. Ⓐ Ⓑ Ⓒ Ⓓ
161. Ⓐ Ⓑ Ⓒ Ⓓ
162. Ⓐ Ⓑ Ⓒ Ⓓ
163. Ⓐ Ⓑ Ⓒ Ⓓ
164. Ⓐ Ⓑ Ⓒ Ⓓ
165. Ⓐ Ⓑ Ⓒ Ⓓ
166. Ⓐ Ⓑ Ⓒ Ⓓ
167. Ⓐ Ⓑ Ⓒ Ⓓ
168. Ⓐ Ⓑ Ⓒ Ⓓ
169. Ⓐ Ⓑ Ⓒ Ⓓ
170. Ⓐ Ⓑ Ⓒ Ⓓ

PRACTICE TEST

TIME: 5 hours

READING

Read the passage below; then answer the nine questions that follow.

WATER

1   The most important source of sediment is earth and rock material carried to the sea by rivers and streams; glaciers and winds may also have transported the same materials. Other sources are volcanic ash and lava, shells and skeletons of organisms, chemical precipitates formed in seawater, and particles from outer space.

2   Water, like molten lava is a most unusual substance because it exists on the surface of the Earth in different physical states. Water may take the form of a solid, liquid, or vapor. There are other substances that exist in a solid and liquid or gaseous state at temperatures normally found at the Earth's surface, but there are fewer substances that occur in all three states.

3   Water is odorless, tasteless, and colorless. It is the only substance known to exist in a natural state as a solid, liquid, or gas on the surface of the Earth. It is a universal solvent. Water does not corrode, rust, burn, or separate into its components easily. It is chemically indestructible. It can corrode almost any metal and erode the most solid rock. A unique property of water is that, when frozen in its solid state, it expands and floats on water. Water has a freezing point of 0°C and a boiling point of 100°C. Water has the capacity to absorb great quantities of heat with relatively little increase in temperature. When distilled, water is a poor conductor of electricity but when salt is added, it is a good conductor of electricity.

4   Sunlight is the source of energy for temperature change, evaporation, and currents for water movement through the atmosphere. Sunlight controls the rate of photosynthesis for all marine plants, which are directly or indirectly the source of food for all marine animals. Migration, breeding, and other behaviors of marine animals are affected by light.

5   Water, as the ocean or sea, is blue because of the molecular scattering of the sunlight. Blue light, being of short wavelength, is scattered more effectively than light of longer wavelengths. Variations in color may be caused by particles suspended in the water, water depth, cloud cover, temperature, and other variable factors. Heavy concentrations of dissolved materials cause a yellowish hue, while algae will cause the water to look green. Heavy populations of plant and animal materials will cause the water to look brown.

1. Based on the information in the passage, what would be the cause of water changing color?

    (A) wind and migration

    (B) sunlight and particles

    (C) wind variations

    (D) freezing water and blue water

2. Which paragraph does not contain important information about water?

    (A) Paragraph 1—the most important source of sediment.

    (B) Paragraph 2—properties of water.

    (C) Paragraph 4—sunlight is a source of energy.

    (D) Paragraph 5—dissolved minerals can change the color of water.

3. Which statement is not a factual in nature?

    (A) Water has three physical states.

    (B) Water changes color.

    (C) Water is the most unusual substance.

    (D) Water temperature is changed by sunlight.

4. The phrase, "Water, like molten lava . . ." means

    (A) water is a precious metal.

    (B) metal may be used as an objective description.

    (C) water is as hard as rock.

    (D) water and lava have similar changeable states.

5. Which of the following lists of topics best organizes the information in the selection?

    (A) I.   Water as vapor

         II. Water as ice

         III. Water as solid

    (B) I.   Properties of seawater

         II. Freezing and boiling points of water

         III. Photosynthesis

         IV. Oceans and seas

    (C) I.   Water as substance

         II. Water's corrosion

         III. Water and plants

         IV. Water and algae coloration

    (D) I.   Water's physical states

         II. Properties of water

         III. Effects of the sun on water

         IV. Reasons for color variation in water

6. According to the passage, what is the most unique property of water?

    (A) Water is odorless, tasteless, and colorless.

    (B) Water exists on the surface of the Earth in three physical states.

    (C) Water is chemically indestructible.

    (D) Water is a poor conductor of electricity.

7. Which of the following best defines the word <u>distilled</u> as it is used in the last sentence of the third paragraph?

    (A) free of salt content

    (B) free of electrical energy

    (C) dehydrated

    (D) containing wine

8. The writer's main purpose in this selection is to

    (A) explain the colors of water.

    (B) examine the effects of the sun on water.

    (C) define the properties of water.

    (D) describe the three physical states of all liquids.

9. The writer of this selection would most likely agree with which of the following statements?

    (A) The properties of water are found in most other liquids on this planet.

    (B) Water should not be consumed in its most natural state.

    (C) Water might be used to serve many different functions.

    (D) Water is too unpredictable for most scientists.

Read the passage below; then answer the seven questions that follow.

THE BEGINNINGS OF THE SUBMARINE

1   A submarine was first used as a military weapon during the American Revolutionary War. The *Turtle*, a one-man submersible designed by an American named David Bushnell and hand-operated by a screw propeller, attempted to sink a British warship in New York Harbor. The plan was to attach a charge of gunpowder to the ship's bottom with screws and explode it with a time fuse, _____ the repeated failures forced the screws through the copper sheathing of the hull of the H.M.S. *Eagle*. The submarine gave up and withdrew, exploding its powder a short distance from the *Eagle*. Although the attack was unsuccessful, it caused the British to _____ defeat and move their blockading ships from the harbor to the outer bay.

2   On February 17, 1864, a Confederate craft, a hand-propelled submersible carrying a crew of eight men, sank a Federal corvette that was blockading Charleston Harbor. The hit was accomplished by a torpedo suspended ahead of the Confederate *Hunley* as she rammed the Union frigate *Housatonic*, and is the first recorded instance of a submarine sinking a warship.

3   The submarine first became a major component in naval warfare during World War I, when Germany demonstrated its full potential. The wholesale sinking of Allied supply ships by the German U-boats almost swung the war in favor of the Central Powers. Then, as now, the submarine's greatest advantage was that it could operate beneath the ocean's surface where detection was difficult. Sinking a submarine was comparatively easy, once it was found—but finding it before it could attack was another matter.

4   During the closing months of World War I, the Allied Submarine Devices Investigation Committee was formed to obtain from science and technology more effective underwater detection equipment. The committee developed a reasonably accurate device for locating a submerged submarine. This device was a trainable hydrophone, which was attached to the bottom of the ASW ship, and used to detect screw noises and other sounds that came from a submarine. Although the committee disbanded after World War I, the British made improvements on the locating device during the interval between the world wars, and named it ASDIC after the committee.

5   American scientists further improved on the device, calling it SONAR, a name derived from letters in the words *so*und *na*vigation *r*anging. The SONAR proved to be the greatest device that was ever invented in the history of navigation.

6   At the end of World War II, the United States improved the snorkel (a device for bringing air to the crew and engines when operating submerged on diesels) and developed the Guppy (short for greater underwater propulsion power), a conversion of the fleet-type submarine of World War II fame. Reducing the surface area, streamlining every protruding object, and enclosing the periscope shears in a streamlined metal fairing changed the superstructure. Performance increased greatly with improved electronic equipment, additional battery capacity, and the addition of the snorkel.

10. Using the two blanks provided in the first paragraph, which pair of words should be inserted to provide the correct meaning to the paragraph?

   (A) except and accept.

   (B) affect and effect.

   (C) insure and ensure.

   (D) there and their.

11. Among the following statements, which one is an opinion of the author?

   (A) The United States improved the snorkel and developed the Guppy.

   (B) During the closing months of World War I, the Allied Submarine Devices Investigation Committee was formed to obtain from science and technology more effective underwater detection equipment.

   (C) On February 17, 1864, a Confederate craft, a hand-propelled submersible carrying a crew of eight men, sank a Federal corvette that was blocking Charleston Harbor.

   (D) SONAR proved to be the greatest device that was ever invented in the history of navigation.

12. The passage implies that one of the most pressing modifications needed for the submarine was to

   (A) streamline its shape.

   (B) enlarge the submarine for accommodating more torpedoes and men.

   (C) reduce the noise caused by the submarine.

   (D) add a snorkel.

13. It is inferred that

   (A) ASDIC was formed to obtain technology for underwater detection.

   (B) ASDIC developed an accurate device for locating submarines.

   (C) the hydrophone was attached to the bottom of the ship.

   (D) ASDIC was formed to develop technology to defend U.S. shipping.

14. SONAR not only picked up the sound of submarines moving through the water but also

    (A) indicated the speed at which the sub was moving.

    (B) gave the location of the submarine.

    (C) indicated the speed of the torpedo.

    (D) placed the submarine within a specified range.

15. According to the passage, the submarine's success was due in part to its ability to

    (A) strike and escape undetected.

    (B) move more swiftly than other vessels.

    (C) submerge to great depths while being hunted.

    (D) run silently.

16. From the passage, one can infer that

    (A) David Bushnell was indirectly responsible for the sinking of the Federal corvette in Charlestown Harbor.

    (B) David Bushnell invented the *Turtle*.

    (C) the *Turtle* was a one-man submarine.

    (D) the *Turtle* sank the USS *Housatonic* on February 18, 1864.

Read the passage below; then answer the eight questions that follow.

IMMIGRATION

1   The influx of immigrants that America had been experiencing slowed during the conflicts with France and England, but the flow increased between 1820 and 1840. Thus, the overall rise in population during these years was due more to incoming foreigners than to a natural, domestically derived increase. Most of the newcomers were from Britain, Germany, and southern Ireland. The Germans usually fared best, since they brought more money and more skills. Discrimination was common in the job market, primarily directed against the Catholics. "Irish Need Not Apply" signs were common. It is fair to say that all immigrants experience discrimination when they arrived in America, however, the persistent labor shortage prevented the natives from totally excluding the

foreign elements. These newcomers huddled in ethnic neighborhoods in the cities, or those who could move on Westward to try their hand at farming.

2   In 1790, five percent of the U.S. population lived in cities of 2,500 or more. By 1860, that figure had risen to 25%. This rapid urbanization created an array of problems.

Sources of Immigration, 1820–1840

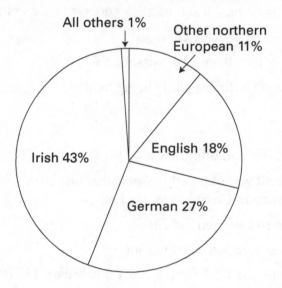

3   The rapid growth in urban areas was not matched by the growth of services, however. Clean water, trash removal, housing, and public transportation all lagged behind, and the wealthy got them first. Bad water and poor sanitation produced poor health, and epidemics of typhoid fever, typhus, and cholera were common. Police and fire protection were usually inadequate and the development of professional police and fire forces was delayed until 1894 when the departments adapted a civil service system to fight corruption.

4   Rapid growth helped to produce a wave of violence in the cities. In New York City in 1834, the Democrats fought the Whigs with such vigor that the state militia had to be called in. New York and Philadelphia witnessed race riots in the mid-1830s, and a New York mob sacked a Catholic convent in 1834. In the 1830s, 115 major incidents of mob violence were recorded. Street crime was common in all major cities.

17. As immigrants arrived in America, they experienced discrimination. People did not want to hire foreigners for local jobs. Therefore,

    (A) no immigrants were hired for positions in America.

    (B) immigrants were hired due to the labor shortage.

    (C) no jobs were available for immigrants.

    (D) some cities had more jobs open to immigrants.

18. A pattern of similarities developed as cities experienced rapid growth which included

    (A) discrimination, unsanitary housing conditions, lack of services, epidemics, and violence.

    (B) better services, clean water, and police protection.

    (C) Irish, German, and English immigrants lived peacefully.

    (D) the adoption of a state militia.

19. The author used an error in reasoning by stating

    (A) rapid growth of cities does not match the growth of services.

    (B) all immigrants experience discrimination when they arrived in America.

    (C) in 1820 and 1840, America experienced a growth in immigrants.

    (D) the civil service system was adapted in 1894.

20. The author's purpose in writing this essay is to

    (A) bring to light the poor treatment of immigrants.

    (B) show the violent effects of overpopulation.

    (C) trace the relationship of immigration to the problems of rapid urban growth.

    (D) dissuade an active life in big cities.

21. Which of the following best defines the word <u>sacked</u> as it is used in the last paragraph?

    (A) robbed

    (B) carried

    (C) trespassed on

    (D) vandalized

22. Which of the following statements best summarizes the main idea of the fourth paragraph?

    (A) Racial tensions caused riots in New York City and Philadelphia.

    (B) The rapid growth in urban population sowed the seeds of violence in U.S. cities.

    (C) Street crimes were far worse in urban areas than race riots and political fights.

    (D) The state militia was responsible for curbing urban violence.

23. Ideas presented in the selection are most influenced by which of the following assumptions?

    (A) Urban life was more or less controllable before the flow of immigration in 1820.

    (B) The British had more skills than the Irish.

    (C) Ethnic neighborhoods had always been a part of American society.

    (D) France and England often had conflicts.

24. According to the graph, from 1820 to 1840

    (A) there were more Irish immigrants than all other nationalities combined.

    (B) the combined number of immigrants from England and Germany exceeded those from Ireland.

    (C) one percent of American immigrants were from Italy.

    (D) there were an equal number of English and German immigrants.

Read the passage below; then answer the three questions that follow.

To receive an "A" on a paper in this class, one must write sophisticated prose. The criteria will be based on the complexity of both content and expression. The grade will require a demonstration of obvious familiarity with primary texts, as well as additional readings of the course and secondary materials and research sources. An effective combination of personal opinion and outside sources will also be required. Proficiency in organizational skills, format, rhetoric, grammar, syntax, and sentence structure is a must. An additional requirement is a thoroughly proofread essay resulting in no distracting mechanical errors, with the possible exception of occasional arguable usage.

25. To receive an "A" grade in the above class, the student must

    (A) turn in a proofread paper with no punctuation errors and demonstrate an understanding of the reading material.

    (B) write an effective paper without mistakes and with an abundance of secondary source materials.

    (C) turn in a thoughtful paper with no corrections as well as demonstrate a proficiency of organizational skills, such as format, rhetoric, and grammar.

    (D) write an intelligent paper without regard for grammar, syntax, or rhetorical strategies, with the possible exception of occasional arguable usage.

26. What does the author mean by "sophisticated prose"?

    (A) a readable text that does not make sense

    (B) a readable text made up of knowledgeable or thoughtful language

    (C) a readable text consisting of pompous or ostentatious language

    (D) a readable text made up of poetic metaphor

27. When the author of the passage refers to the "primary texts," he means

    (A) the reference materials, such as the dictionary, encyclopedia, thesaurus, etc.

    (B) the primary note pages, works cited page, or preliminary rough draft page.

    (C) the source or principal text in the assignment.

    (D) the first text written about a certain subject.

Read the passage below; then answer the four questions that follow.

Language not only expresses an individual's ideology, it also sets perimeters while it persuades and influences the discourse in the community that hears and interprets its meaning. Therefore, the language of failure should not be present in the learning environment (i.e., the classroom) because it will have a prohibitive impact on the students' desire to learn as well as a negative influence on the students' self-esteem. The *Oxford English Dictionary* defines *failure* as a fault, a shortcoming, a lack of success, a person who turns out unsuccessfully, becoming insolvent, etc. We as educators might well ask ourselves if this is the sort of doctrine that we want to permeate our classrooms. Perhaps our own University motto, *Mens agitat molem* ("mind moves the mass," from the writings of Virgil), will help us discover if, indeed, the concepts of failure are really the types of influences we wish to introduce to impressionable new students. Is the mind capable of moving a mass when it is already convinced it cannot? One must remain aware that individuals acquire knowledge at independent rates of speed. Certainly no one would suggest that one infant "failed" the art of learning to walk because she acquired the skill two months behind her infant counterpart. Would anyone suggest that infant number one *failed* walking? Of course not. What would a mentor project to either toddler were he to suggest that a slower acquisition of walking skills implied failure? Yet we as educators feel the need to suggest student A failed due to the slower procurement of abstract concepts than student B. It is absolutely essential to shift the learning focus from failure to success.

28. Which of the following statements best conveys the meaning of the passage?

    (A) Learning is something that happens at different speeds and is, therefore, natural.

    (B) Instructors need to be sensitive to students' individual needs.

    (C) Instructors need to shift the educational focus from failure to success in learning environments.

    (D) Failure is a potential hazard in the classroom and should be avoided at all costs.

29. As stated in the context of the passage, what does <u>motto</u> most nearly mean?

    (A) Latin

    (B) maxim

    (C) rhetoric

    (D) sophomore

30. According to the passage, what will have a negative effect on student self-esteem?

    (A) the rhetoric of diction

    (B) the slower procurement of abstract concepts

    (C) the learning focus from failure to success

    (D) the language of failure

31. According to the passage, what does language do besides aid individual expression?

(A) It establishes individual thought and tells of individual philosophies.

(B) It paints visual images and articulates individual declaration.

(C) It suggests individual axioms and community philosophy.

(D) It persuades and influences the discourse in the community that hears and interprets its meaning.

Read the passage below; then answer the five questions that follow.

1   Frederick Douglass was born Frederick Augustus Washington Bailey in 1817 to a white father and a slave mother. Frederick was raised by his grandmother on a Maryland plantation until he was eight. It was then that he was sent to Baltimore by his owner to be a servant to the Auld family. Mrs. Auld recognized Frederick's intellectual acumen and defied the law of the state by teaching him to read and write. When Mr. Auld warned that education would make the boy unfit for slavery, Frederick sought to continue his education in the streets. When his master died, Frederick, who was only sixteen years of age, was returned to the plantation to work in the fields. Later, he was hired out to work in the shipyards in Baltimore as a ship caulker. He plotted an escape but was discovered before he could get away. It took five years before he made his way to New York City and then to New Bedford, Massachusetts, eluding slave hunters by changing his name to Douglass.

2   At an 1841 anti-slavery meeting in Massachusetts, Douglass was invited to give a talk about his experiences under slavery. His impromptu speech was so powerful and so eloquent that it thrust him into a career as an agent for the Massachusetts Anti-Slavery Society. Douglass wrote his autobiography in 1845, primarily to counter those who doubted his authenticity as a former slave. This work became a classic in American literature and a primary source about slavery from the point of view of a slave. Douglass went on a two-year speaking tour abroad to avoid recapture by his former owner and to win new friends for the abolition movement.

3   He returned with funds to purchase his freedom and to start his own anti-slavery newspaper. He became a consultant to Abraham Lincoln and throughout Reconstruction fought doggedly for full civil rights for freedmen; he also supported the women's rights movement.

32. According to the passage, Douglass's writing of his autobiography was motivated by

    (A) the desire to make money for the anti-slavery movement.

    (B) his desire to become a publisher.

    (C) his interest in authenticating his life as a slave.

    (D) his desire to educate people about the horrors of slavery.

33. The central idea of the passage is that Douglass

    (A) was instrumental in changing the laws regarding the education of slaves.

    (B) was one of the most eminent human rights leaders of the nineteenth century.

    (C) was a personal friend and confidant to a president.

    (D) wrote a classic in American literature.

34. According to the author of this passage, Mrs. Auld taught Douglass to read because

    (A) Douglass wanted to go to school like the other children.

    (B) she recognized his natural ability.

    (C) she wanted to comply with the laws of the state.

    (D) he needed to be able to read so that he might work in the home.

35. The title that best expresses the ideas of this passage is

    (A) The History of the Anti-Slavery Movement in America.

    (B) The Outlaw Frederick Douglass.

    (C) Reading: A Window to the World of Abolition.

    (D) Frederick Douglass's Contributions to Freedom.

36. In the context of the passage, impromptu most nearly means

    (A) unprepared.

    (B) nervous.

    (C) angry.

    (D) loud.

Read the passage below; then answer the three questions that follow.

During a class on theories and methods of education, the teaching apprentice initiated the discussion in a clear and well-prepared manner. To _____ the lecture topic, the teaching apprentice utilized overhead transparencies of both lexicon and abstract representation to better _____ the theories behind various pedagogical concepts. The class culminated whereby students established enthymemes extrapolated from the class discussion. The class maintained integrity and continuity.

37. Which of these grouped words, if inserted *in order* into the passage's blank lines, would address the logical sequencing of the narrative?

    (A) refute; criticize

    (B) conflate; discern

    (C) undermine; explain

    (D) support; illustrate

38. As used in the sentence, <u>pedagogical</u> most nearly means

    (A) academic.

    (B) abstract.

    (C) meaningless.

    (D) obtuse.

39. The passage suggests that the author's classroom experience was

    (A) a needless waste of time and energy.

    (B) intelligible and pragmatic.

    (C) haphazard and disorderly.

    (D) too advanced and complicated.

Read the passage below; then answer the three questions that follow.

The early decades of the fifteenth century were a period in our history when English took a "great (linguistic) vowel shift" by redistributing the vowel pronunciation and configuration. Each vowel changed its sound quality, but the distinction between one vowel and the next was maintained. There was a restructuring of the sounds and patterns of communication, as well. One has to conclude that a concurrent stress and exhilaration was occurring within the perimeters of the literate society as well. Musicians, artists, poets, and authors all must have relished the new freedom and experimentation that was now possible with the new-found linguistic shifts.

40. The passage tells about

(A) a shift in vowel pronunciation and configuration.

(B) a fifteenth-century renaissance for musicians, artists, poets, and authors.

(C) a new-found linguistic freedom from conventional sound and linguistic structure.

(D) various vowel stresses and their effect on artistic expression.

41. What is the meaning of the word <u>linguistic</u> as used in the passage?

(A) artistic freedom

(B) verbal or rhetorical

(C) social or expressive

(D) vowel configuration

42. Because "each vowel changed its sound quality,"

(A) there was a restructuring of the sounds and patterns of communication.

(B) language could never be spoken in the same way again.

(C) artists had to develop new means of expression.

(D) communication went through a divergent change of status and culture.

Read the passage below; then answer the four questions that follow.

Lead poisoning is considered by health authorities to be the most common and devastating environmental disease of young children. According to studies, it affects 15% to 20% of urban children and from 50% to 75% of inner-city, poor children. As a result of a legal settlement in July 1991, all California MediCal-eligible children, ages one through five, will now be routinely screened annually for lead poisoning. Experts estimate that more than 50,000 cases will be detected in California because of the newly mandated tests. This will halt at an early stage a disease that leads to learning disabilities and life-threatening disorders.

43. Lead poisoning among young children, if not detected early, can lead to
    (A) physical disabilities.
    (B) heart disease.
    (C) liver disease.
    (D) learning disabilities and death.

44. The new mandate to screen all young children for lead poisoning is required of
    (A) all young children in California.
    (B) all children with learning disabilities.
    (C) all MediCal-eligible children, ages one through five, in California.
    (D) all minority children in inner cities.

45. The percentages indicate that more cases of lead poisoning are found among
    (A) children in rural areas.
    (B) inner-city children.
    (C) immigrant children.
    (D) upper-middle-class children.

46. The ultimate goal of the newly mandated tests is to
    (A) bring more monies into inner-city medical programs.
    (B) bring more health care professionals into California's inner cities.
    (C) halt at an early stage a disease that leads to learning disabilities and life-threatening disorders.
    (D) screen more test subjects to develop more accurate statistical data.

Read the passage below; then answer the two questions that follow.

America's national bird, the mighty bald eagle, is being threatened by a new menace. Once decimated by hunters and loss of habitat, this newest danger is suspected to be from the intentional poisoning by livestock ranchers. Authorities have found animal carcasses injected with restricted pesticides. These carcasses are suspected to have been placed to attract and kill predators such as the bald eagle in an effort to preserve young grazing animals. It appears that the eagle is being threatened again by the consummate predator, humans.

47. One can conclude from this passage that
    (A) the pesticides used are beneficial to the environment.
    (B) ranchers believe that killing the eagles will protect their ranches.
    (C) ranchers must obtain licenses to use illegal pesticides.
    (D) poisoning eagles is good for livestock.

48. The author's attitude is one of
    (A) uncaring observation.
    (B) concerned interest.
    (C) uniform acceptance.
    (D) suspicion.

Read the passage below; then answer the six questions that follow.

Life in seventeenth-century England was tempestuous indeed. It was a time when religious and secular confrontations resulted in new social abstractions, paradoxes, and ironies. The poet-pastor Robert Herrick (1591–1674) illustrates the ability of lyric poetry to serve not only as an adornment of the era, but as social communiqué, as well. Herrick's Mayday celebration poem "Corinna's Going A-Maying" serves as both an argument against conservative religious dogma and as a response to specific Puritan manifestos. Herrick incorporates abundant Greco-Roman tropes into "Corinna" in order to construct a stylized response to Puritanism based upon traditional structure, symmetry, and thematic representation.

49. The author's attitude toward the subject is one of

    (A) lethargy.

    (B) apathy.

    (C) objectivity.

    (D) intensity.

50. The passage fundamentally suggests that

    (A) Puritanism is based upon a traditional structure, symmetry, and thematic representation.

    (B) lyric poetry has the ability to serve not only as an adornment of an era, but also as social communiqué.

    (C) life in seventeenth-century England was tempestuous indeed.

    (D) the seventeenth century was a time of religious and secular confrontations, resulting in new social abstractions, paradoxes, and ironies.

51. As used in the passage, the word <u>trope</u> most nearly means

    (A) a group of people, animals, etc., such as a herd, a flock, a band, and so on.

    (B) a style of writing in the Greek or Roman language.

    (C) a desire to travel to Greece or Rome.

    (D) the use of a word in a figurative sense; a figure of speech; figurative language.

52. The writer's reference to a poetic form suggests

    (A) seventeenth-century England was in social turmoil.

    (B) Puritan manifesto was in social turmoil

    (C) religious dogma contributes to intellectual stagnation.

    (D) lyric poetry can serve as a vehicle to express social commentary.

53. The writer describes the social fabric of seventeenth-century England as tempestuous, which means

    (A) dogma challenges social order.

    (B) England is a subgenre of the lyrical poetic style.

    (C) England is highly charged and emotional.

    (D) social and political disobedience.

54. The statement that best expresses the main idea of the passage is

    (A) Robert Herrick used lyrical poetic style to describe a social era and offer social commentary.

    (B) The 1600s, in England were dangerous and chaotic.

    (C) Robert Herrick's poem "Corianna's Going A-Maying" was one of his most celebrated poems.

    (D) Puritanism as a religious construct was constraining social thought.

Read the passage below; then answer the six questions that follow.

A Critic can be equivalent to "a person who pronounces judgment; especially a *Censurer.*" Since the late sixteenth century, the title of Critic has embodied implied meanings such as "professionalism" and "a person *skilled* in textual criticism." Thereby, the title insinuates a distinction of hierarchy among laborers, craftsmen, and the "working class" in general. "Censure" has etymological connotations that date back to the late Middle Ages, "critical recension or revision (along with) expression(s) of disapproval, to give opinion, assess critically, find fault, reprove, blame, pronounce sentence," and "condemnatory (especially ecclesiastical) judgment, opinion, correction," which all furthermore suggest a rather antagonistic posture in relationship to the Humanities. The position of critic is tenuous, as they can serve both as censure or social analyst and commentator. Subsequently, the word is loaded with negative innuendoes, but also innuendoes that denote authority, repression, and judicial propriety. In essence, the Critic who chooses to take the point-of-view of the Censure, sits on the mountaintop, not for a better view of literature, but to establish a false sense of superiority over it in relationship to the Author (as well as the reader for that matter).

55. The passage suggests that

    (A) critics are good for the social order.

    (B) the position of critic is tenuous as they can serve both as censure or social analyst and commentator.

    (C) critics attempt to establish a false sense of superiority over the author and the reader as well.

    (D) humanitarians do not make good critics as they are too emotional and not callous or impartial enough.

56. The passage indicates that the art of criticism

    (A) is a modern phenomenon.

    (B) dates back to the Middle Ages.

    (C) is a thought-provoking entity.

    (D) began at around the same time as the Civil War.

57. Which of the following would make the best title for the passage you just read?

    (A) Critical Analysis Ruins Literature for the Rest of Us

    (B) Critics Assume a False Superiority Thereby Rendering Critical Judgment Null and Void

    (C) The Implications and Connotations of the Critic as Author

    (D) Criticism is Synonymous with Censorship

58. What does the term <u>etymological</u> most nearly mean as it is used in the passage?

    (A) the history of the Middle Ages

    (B) the history of a word

    (C) the history of critical analysis

    (D) the history of literature

59. Which of the following statements is an accurate summary of the passage?

    (A) Critics are positive and supportive of the writer and his work.

    (B) Critics are always arrogant and reflect an "air of superiority."

    (C) A critic, as a censurer understands the delicate balance inherent in the role.

    (D) A critic is an effective approach to literary criticism.

60. The writer of the passage wants the reader to believe that a critic, as censurer,

    (A) reviews literary work in a fair and impartial manner.

    (B) expresses a populist point of view of an author's work.

    (C) provides objective reviews of literary works.

    (D) is viewed as a negative person who exerts his own opinions on literary art.

LANGUAGE ARTS

Read the passage below, written in the style of a newspaper editorial; then answer the five questions that follow.

[1]The zoning regulations of Westown have long been a thorn in the side of local real estate developers. [2]The authors of those regulations apparently believed that their regulations would be appropriate in perpetuity, because they _____ to amend. [3]The result is a growing area of blight bounded on the north by Bradley Avenue and on the east by Randolph Street.

[4]This coming Wednesday the Westown's city council has a chance to bring its zoning practices into the twenty-first century. [5]The _____ votes will come from Council members Putman, Beckett, and Reis. [6]The votes of Putman and Beckett in particular will be of interest to their constituents, because the residents of their wards would stand to gain a great deal from rezoning. [7]The proposed changes would bring the Fourth Ward some much-needed commerce in the currently run-down Randolph-MacKenzie area and would help _____ the Fifth Ward's steady population loss. [8]Although each of these self-styled "progressives" have displayed reluctance to vote for anything that would spur development in the recent past, both have strong opposition in the upcoming election and would do well to consider how their votes on this issue will impact the results of that election.

61. Which of the following changes is needed in the passage above?

    (A) Part 1: Change "have" to "has"

    (B) Part 4: Change "Westown's" to "Westown"

    (C) Part 8: Change the comma after "past" to a semicolon

    (D) Part 8: Change "how" to "that"

62. Which of the following words would be the best to insert into the blank in Part 5?

    (A) deliberate

    (B) divided

    (C) decisive

    (D) doubtful

63. Which of the following words would be the best to insert into the blank in Part 7?

    (A) alleviate

    (B) accelerate

    (C) excoriate

    (D) exonerate

64. Which of the numbered parts should be revised to correct an error in verb form?

    (A) Part 3

    (B) Part 5

    (C) Part 6

    (D) Part 8

65. Which of the following phrases, inserted into the blank in Part 2, would make sense and would be free of errors?

    (A) made the regulations very easy

    (B) ensured that the provisions would be difficult

    (C) made them almost impossible

    (D) said the zoning ordinances will be hard

Read the passage below, written in the style of a case study for a college education textbook; then answer the six questions that follow.

[1]DeMarco was asked if he had read any of the books that were on display in Mrs. W's classroom. [2]He answered that he had read none of them yet, although he usually keeps one or more in his desk.

[3]Nevertheless, the researcher did see him respond positively to the first classroom reading experience of the year. [4]Mrs. W was reading Louis Sachar's *Sideways Stories from Wayside School* while the children, each of whom had a copy of the book, were silently reading along. [5]Like nearly all of the class, DeMarco was laughing in all the right places. [6]The researcher has since noticed that he grasps and comprehends just about anything well when it is read by a competent reader, whether a teacher or an advanced fellow student.

[7]_____ [8]The class writes almost daily in a "Small Moments Journal," in which they are to <u>record</u>, in a few sentences and perhaps a picture, memorable events in their lives. [9]Mrs. W has spent <u>considerable</u> time

prompting the students to write down topics, with the result that some students have well over 100 topics listed so far. ¹⁰DeMarco, through the last day he was observed, had seven. ¹¹He had written only two entries in his journal, both about a visit two years ago to his relatives in Mississippi. ¹²Like many of his classmate's accounts of their <u>comings and goings</u>, his writing lacks detail and personality, but most others have written <u>appreciably</u> more. ¹³Asked follow-up questions about the events he has written about, his answers were _____.

66. Which of the following sentences, used in place of the blank labeled Part 7, would best make a transition to the new paragraph?

    (A) Another topic of interest was the study of DeMarco's writing ability.

    (B) Moreover, DeMarco's writing shows no enthusiasm.

    (C) DeMarco's writing, however, shows no spark at all.

    (D) Consequently, it is advisable that we look at DeMarco's writing.

67. Which of the numbered parts should be revised to reduce its unnecessary repetition?

    (A) Part 3

    (B) Part 5

    (C) Part 6

    (D) Part 8

68. Which of the numbered parts should be revised to correct an error in sentence structure?

    (A) Part 2

    (B) Part 9

    (C) Part 10

    (D) Part 13

69. Which of the following changes is needed in the passage?

    (A) Part 4: Change *Sideways Stories from Wayside School* to "Sideways Stories from Wayside School"

    (B) Part 11: Change "had" to "has"

    (C) Part 11: Change "journal" to "Journal"

    (D) Part 12: Change "classmate's" to "classmates'"

70. Which of the underlined words or phrases in the third paragraph should be replaced by more precise or appropriate words?

    (A) <u>record</u>

    (B) <u>considerable</u>

    (C) <u>comings and goings</u>

    (D) <u>appreciably</u>

71. Which of the following words would be the best to insert into the blank in Part 13?

    (A) elucidating

    (B) electrifying

    (C) expansive

    (D) evasive

Read the passage below, written in the style of a history of science college textbook; then answer the six questions that follow.

[1]The Tuskegee Experiment's true nature had to be hidden from the subjects to ensure their cooperation. [2]The sharecroppers' grossly disadvantaged lot in life made them easy to manipulate. [3]Pleased at the prospect of free medical care—almost none of them had ever seen a doctor before—these unsophisticated and trusting men became the dupes in what James Jones, author of the excellent history on the subject, *Bad Blood,* identified as "the longest nontherapeutic experiment on human beings in medical history".

[4]The study was meant to discover how syphilis <u>effected</u> African Americans as opposed to whites—the theory being that whites experienced more neurological complications from syphilis <u>whereas</u> African Americans were more <u>susceptible</u> to cardiovascular damage. [5]_____
_____ [6]Although the scientists _____ the study as one of great scientific merit, from the <u>outset</u> its actual benefits were hazy. [7]It took almost forty years before someone involved in the study took a hard and honest look at the end results, he reported that "nothing learned will prevent, find, or cure a single case of infectious syphilis or bring us closer to our basic mission of controlling venereal disease in the United States." [8]When the media learns of the experiment in 1972, the CBS news anchor Harry Reasoner called it a project that "used human beings as laboratory animals in a long and inefficient study of how long it takes syphilis to kill someone."

72. Which of the following sentences, used in place of the blank labeled Part 5, would be most consistent with the writer's purpose and intended audience?

    (A) If the theory had been proven, much would have changed in the clinical treatment of syphilis.

    (B) How this knowledge would have changed the clinical treatment of syphilis is uncertain.

    (C) On the other hand, neurological complications were much more important to the scientists.

    (D) We will never know what the racist scientists of the 1920s were thinking when they devised this theory.

73. Which of the underlined words or phrases in the second paragraph should be replaced by more precise or appropriate words?

    (A) effected

    (B) whereas

    (C) susceptible

    (D) outset

74. Which of the numbered parts should be revised to correct a nonstandard use of a comma?

    (A) Part 2

    (B) Part 3

    (C) Part 7

    (D) Part 8

75. Which of the following changes is needed in the first paragraph?

    (A) Part 1: Change "experiment's" to "experiments"

    (B) Part 2: Change "easy to manipulate" to "easily manipulated"

    (C) Part 3: Change "had" to "has"

    (D) Part 3: Move the period at the end inside the quotation mark

76. Which of the numbered sentences contains nonstandard use of a verb form?

    (A) Part 2

    (B) Part 3

    (C) Part 6

    (D) Part 8

77. Which of the following words would be the best to insert into the blank in Part 6?

    (A) touted

    (B) tempted

    (C) tantalized

    (D) trumped

Read the passage below, written in the style of a sociology textbook; then answer the seven questions that follow.

[1]Before the Europeans arrived, animism and spirit worship was the hallmark of Timorese belief in a superior force. [2]The great Hindu, Buddhist, and Islamic kingdoms that dominated South and Southeast Asia had not taken root in Timor. [3]The island's geographic location, which was far from the major ports of Asia, and its subsequent lack of commercial activity, placed it off the beaten track for traders and proselytizers. [4]The exceptions being sandalwood and later slave trade.

[5]All that changed with the arrival of the Europeans. [6]By the late 1500s Dominican friars from Portugal had established a mission on Timor, _____ they made only modest headway in converting the Timorese to Christianity. [7]Although the Portuguese were in Timor for centuries they had little positive influence on Timorese culture until after World War II. [8]For years the local people consistently resisted Portugal's attempts to take control of their island, and some of the Dominican missionaries who were posted there supported them in this effort. [9]It was not until Portugal considered granting East Timor its independence that Catholicism began to be accepted among the people, and _____ it was not until the Indonesian invasion in 1975 that large numbers of Timorese embraced the Catholic faith. [10]Indonesian law requires citizens to have a religious affiliation. [11]The Catholic Church was the only organization that the Indonesian government in Timor allowed relative freedom.

[12]Timorese also found the Church a source of support during the guerrilla war against the Indonesians. [13]Timorese fled to the highlands to escape Indonesian rule, and their families were often relocated in camps far from their villages to prevent them from lending assistance to the guerrillas. [14]The Church saw the _____ misery of the people and provided support and comfort. [15]Membership in the Catholic Church grew dramatically from 1975 to 1999 as the Timorese people came to rely on it to protect them and to help them locate missing family members. [16]Today 90% of East Timor's population is Catholic, although many Timorese Catholics include some aspects of animism in their beliefs.

78. Read the following sentence:

    "The priests and nuns of the church provided health care and education to the Timorese during that chaotic period."

    In which of the following locations in the third paragraph should this sentence be placed?

    (A) Before Part 12
    (B) Before Part 13
    (C) Before Part 15
    (D) Before Part 16

79. The method of organization for the second and third paragraphs, respectively, is

    (A) chronological order; problem and solution
    (B) chronological order; cause and effect
    (C) order of importance; chronological order
    (D) comparison and contrast; cause and effect

80. Which of the numbered parts should be revised to correct a nonstandard sentence structure?

    (A) Part 2
    (B) Part 4
    (C) Part 7
    (D) Part 8

81. Which of the following changes is needed in the second paragraph?

    (A)   Part 7: Insert comma after "centuries"

    (B)   Part 8: Change "who" after "missionaries" to "whom"

    (C)   Part 9: Change "its" to "their"

    (D)   Part 11: Capitalize "government"

82. Which words or phrases would, if inserted *in order* into the blanks in the second paragraph, help the reader understand the logical sequence of the writer's ideas?

    (A)   however; therefore

    (B)   and so; in those circumstances

    (C)   however; even then

    (D)   but; even then

83. Which of the numbered parts should be revised to correct a nonstandard verb form?

    (A)   Part 1

    (B)   Part 3

    (C)   Part 10

    (D)   Part 16

84. Which of the following words would be the best to insert into the blank in Part 14?

    (A)   alluring

    (B)   abject

    (C)   objective

    (D)   optimistic

Read the passage below, written in the style of a popular magazine; then answer the five questions that follow.

[1]The Lincoln Cent were first struck in 1909 to celebrate the 100th. Anniversary of the birth of Abraham Lincoln, our 16th President. [2]Designed by Victor D. Brenner, the coin carried the motto "In God We Trust"—the first time it appeared on this denomination coin. [3]It is interesting that the law for the motto was passed during Lincoln's administration as president. [4]Though we might not think so at first glance, the lowly Cent is a fitting memorial for the great man whose profile graces this most common coin of the realm, and a tolerable symbol for the nation whose commerce it serves.

[5]The obverse has the profile of Lincoln as he looked during the trying years of the War Between the States. [6]Faced with the immense problems of a divided nation, the prevention of the split between North and South was difficult. [7]"A house divided against itself cannot stand," he warned the nation. [8]With the outbreak of war at Fort Sumter. Lincoln was saddened to see his beloved country caught up in the senseless war in which father fought against son, brother against brother. [9]Throughout America, war captured the attention of people: the woman who saved the lives of the wounded, the soldier waiting to go into battle, the bewildered child trying hard to understand the sound of guns. [10]Lincoln stood on the broad, silent battlefield at Gettysburg in 1863 to dedicate the site as a national cemetery. [11]Gettysburg had been the scene of some of the most bitter fighting of the war and had ended in a Union victory.

[12]In his special address at Gettysburg, he called upon the American people to end the war. [13]His words boomed out over the large audience before him: [14]"It is rather for us [the living] to be here dedicated to the great task remaining before us—[15]that from these honored dead we take increased devotion to that cause for which they gave the last full measure of devotion; that we here highly resolve that these dead shall not have died in vain; that this nation under God, shall have a new birth of freedom; and that government of the people, by the people and for the people, shall not perish from the earth."

[16]Barely a month before the end of the war, Lincoln took the oath of office a secondly time as President. [17]With the war still raging, his inaugural address took on added meaning: [18] "With malice toward none, with charity for all, with firmness in the right as God gives us to see the right, let us strive on to finish

the work we are in, to bind up the nation's wounds, to care for him who shall have _____ the battle and for his widow and his orphan, to do all which may achieve and cherish a just and lasting peace among ourselves and with all nations."

85. Which of the following changes is needed in the passages above?

(A) Part 1: Change "were" to "was."

(B) Part 3: Change "was" to "were."

(C) Part 7: Change "warned" to "warns."

(D) Part 12: Change "he" to "we."

86. Which of the following changes is needed in the third paragraph?

(A) Part 16: Change "end" to "climax."

(B) Part 16: Change "secondly" to "second."

(C) Part 17: Change "With" to "Of."

(D) Part 17: Change "on" to "in."

87. Which of the following changes is needed in the second paragraph?

(A) Part 5: Change "has" to "had."

(B) Part 6: Change "the prevention of the split between North and South was difficult" to "Lincoln found it difficult to prevent the split between North and South."

(C) Part 9: Change "waiting" to "waited."

(D) Part 10: Change "site" to "sight."

88. Which of the following sentences is a nonstandard sentence?

(A) Part 2

(B) Part 4

(C) Part 8

(D) Part 11

89. Which of the following words would be the best to insert into the blank in Part 18?

(A) beleaguered

(B) borne

(C) opposed

(D) obfuscated

Read the passage below, written in the style of a history of science textbook; then answer the five questions that follow.

[1]Dr. Robert Goddard, at one time a physics professor at Clark University, Worcester, Massachusetts, was largely responsible for the sudden interest in rockets back in the twenties. [2]When Dr. Goddard first started his experiments with rockets, no related technical information was available. [3]He started a new science, industry, and field of engineering. [4]Through his scientific experiments, he pointed the way to the development of rockets as we know them today. [5]The Smithsonian Institution agreed to finance his experiments in the early 1920's. [6]From these experiments he wrote a paper titled "A Method of Reaching Extreme Altitudes," in which he outlined a space rocket of the step (multistage) principle, _____ capable of reaching the moon.

[7]Goddard discovered that with a properly shaped, smooth, tapered nozzle he could increase the ejection velocity eight times with the same weight of fuel. [8]This would not only drive a rocket eight times faster, but 64 times farther, according to his theory. [9]Early in his experiments he found that solid-fuel rockets would not give him the high power or the duration of power needed for a dependable supersonic motor capable of extreme altitudes. [10]Using liquid fuel, he finally launched a successful rocket in 1926.

[11]It attained an altitude of 184 feet and a speed of 60 m.p.h. [12]This seems small as compared to present-day speeds and heights of missile flights, but instead of trying to achieve speed or altitude at this time, Dr. Goddard was trying to develop a dependable rocket motor.

[13]Dr. Goddard later was the first to fire a rocket that reached a speed faster than the speed of sound. [14]He was first to develop a gyroscopic steering <u>thing</u> for rockets. [15]The first to use vanes in the jet stream for rocket stabilization during <u>the initial phase</u> of a rocket flight. [16]And he was first to patent the idea of step rockets. [17]After proving on paper and in <u>actual</u> tests that a rocket can travel in a vacuum, he developed the mathematical theory of rocket propulsion

and rocket flight, including basic designs for long-range rockets. [18]All of his information was available to military men before World War II, but evidently its immediate use did not seem applicable. [19]Near the end of World War II we started intense <u>work</u> on rocket-powered guided missiles, using the experiments and developments of Dr. Goddard and the American Rocket Society.

90. Which of the following should be changed to reflect correct punctuation in the first paragraph?

   (A) Part 1: Remove commas after "Goddard" and after "Massachusetts."

   (B) Part 2: Remove the comma after "rockets."

   (C) Part 4: Put a comma in after "rockets."

   (D) Part 6: Remove the comma after "principle."

91. Which of the following words would be the best to insert into the blank in Part 6?

   (A) hypothetically

   (B) holistically

   (C) theoretically

   (D) theologically

92. Which of the following changes is needed in the passage above?

   (A) Part 5: Change "1920's" to "1920s."

   (B) Part 3: Change "and" to "or."

   (C) Part 8: Change "times" to "fold."

   (D) Part 11: Change "attained" to "aspired."

93. Which of the following parts of the third paragraph is a nonstandard sentence?

   (A) Part 14

   (B) Part 15

   (C) Part 16

   (D) Part 17

94. Which of the underlined words in the fourth paragraph should be replaced by more precise or appropriate words?

   (A) thing

   (B) the initial phase

   (C) actual

   (D) work

Read the passage below, written in the style of an editorial; then answer the five questions that follow.

[1]We've grown accustomed to seeing this working woman hanging from the subway strap during commuting hours. [2]We may refer disparagingly to her tailored suit and little tie, but we no longer visualize her in a house dress with her hair uncombed. [3]The woman who leaves her children to go to work in the morning is no longer a pariah in her community or her family. [4]Her paycheck is more than pin money; it buys essential family staples and often supports the entire family. [5]But she is the only _____ of the increasing presence of women in the workplace.

[6]The situation for men has also changed for the better as a result of women's massive entry into the work force. [7]Men who would once have felt unrelenting pressure to remain with one firm and climb the career ladder are often freed up to change careers in midlife by a second income. [8]They enjoy greatest intimacy and involvement with their children.

[9]The benefits for business are also readily apparent. [10]No senior manager in the country would deny that the huge generation of women who entered management seven or eight years ago has functioned superbly, often outperforming men.

[11]Yet the prevailing message from the media on the subject of women and business is one filled with pessimism. [12]We hear about women leaving their employers in the lurch when they go on maternity leave. [13]Or we hear the flip side, that women are overly committed to their careers and neglectful of their families. [14]And in fact, it is true that problems arising from womens new work force role do exist, side by side with the benefits.

[15]The problems hurt business as well as individuals and their families, affordable quality childcare, for one example, is still a distant dream. [16]Some women are distracted at work, and men who would have felt secure about their children when their wives were home are also anxious and distracted. [17]Distraction also impedes the productivity of some high-achieving women with the birth of their first child and causes some to depart with the birth of their second.

95. Which of the following sentences displays a nonstandard placement of a modifying phrase?

   (A) Part 1

   (B) Part 3

   (C) Part 6

   (D) Part 7

96. Which of the following words would be the best to insert into the blank in Part 5?

   (A) beneficiary

   (B) benefactor

   (C) opponent

   (D) advocate

97. Which of the following sentences displays a nonstandard use of a comparative form?

   (A) Part 4

   (B) Part 8

   (C) Part 10

   (D) Part 13

98. Which of the following changes is needed in the passage above?

   (A) Part 1: Change "We've" to "We're."

   (B) Part 9: Change "are" to "is."

   (C) Part 14: Change "womens" to "women's."

   (D) Part 17: Change "impedes" to "impede."

99. Which of the following sentences is a nonstandard sentence?

    (A) Part 14

    (B) Part 15

    (C) Part 16

    (D) Part 17

Read the passage below, written in the style of a student essay; then answer the four questions that follow.

[1]In the past 30 years, television has become a very popular pastime for almost everyone. [2]From the time she places the baby in her jumpseat in front of the television until the time the senior citizen in the retirement home watches Vanna White turn the letters on "Wheel of Fortune," Americans spend endless hours in front of the "boob tube." [3]How did we get to be this way?

[4]When my mother was a little girl, what did children do to entertain themselves? [5]They played. [6]Their games usually involved social interaction with other children as well as _____ creating entertainment for themselves. [7]They also developed hobbies like woodworking and sewing. [8]Today, few children really know how to play with each other or entertain themselves. [9]Instead, they sit in front of the television, glued to cartoons that are senseless and often violent. [10]Even if they watch educational programs like "Sesame Street," they don't really have to do anything but watch and listen to what the answer to the question is.

[11]Teenagers, also, use television as a way of avoiding doing things that will be helping them mature. [12]How many kids does much homework anymore? [13]Why not? [14]Because they work part-time jobs and come home from work tired and relax in front of the television that's why.

100. Which of the following sentences uses a nonstandard verb form?

    (A) Part 4

    (B) Part 7

    (C) Part 8

    (D) Part 12

101. Which of the following words would be the best to insert into the blank in Part 6?

(A) inspiringly

(B) instinctively

(C) inherently

(D) imaginatively

102. Which of the following sentences in the passage is nonstandard?

(A) Part 2

(B) Part 7

(C) Part 10

(D) Part 14

103. Which of the following changes is needed?

(A) Part 1: Change "has become" to "is."

(B) Part 2: Change "she" to "the mother."

(C) Part 2: Change "watches" to "watched."

(D) Part 4: Change "When" to "Being that."

Read the passage below, written in the style of an anthropology textbook; then answer the three questions that follow.

[1]Actually, the term "Native American" is incorrect. [2]Indians migrated to this continent from other areas, just earlier than Europeans did. [3]The ancestors of the Anasazi—Indians of the four-state area of Colorado, New Mexico, Utah, and Arizona—probably crossed from Asia into Alaska. [4]About 25,000 years ago, while the continental land bridge still existed. [5]This land bridge arched across the Bering Strait in the last Ice Age. [6]About A.D. 500 the ancestors of the Anasazi moved onto the Mesa Verde, a high plateau in the desert country of Colorado. [7]The Wetherills, five brothers who ranched in the area, are generally given credit for the first exploration of the ruins in the 1870s and 1880s. [8]There were some 50,000 Anasazi thriving in the four-corners area by the 1200s A.D. [9]At their _____, A.D. 700 to 1300, the Anasazi had established widespread communities and built thousands of sophisticated structures—cliff dwellings, pueblos, and kivas. [10]They even engaged in trade with Indians in surrounding regions by exporting pottery and other goods.

104. Which of the following is a nonstandard sentence?

(A) Part 1

(B) Part 2

(C) Part 4

(D) Part 5

105. Which of the following words would be the best to insert into the blank in Part 9?

(A) polemic

(B) gestalt

(C) zenith

(D) zeitgeist

106. Which of the following draws attention away from the main idea of the paragraph?

(A) Part 3

(B) Part 4

(C) Part 7

(D) Part 8

Read the passage below, written in the style of a student letter to a college newspaper; then answer the five questions that follow.

[1]The dismissal of Dr. Dennis Ruoff is a travesty of justice. [2]It is not a good feeling to know that a tenured professor can be hounded out of his post just because he disagrees with the board of regents. [3]True, his was the only negative vote on the curriculum issue pushed by the university board of regents. [4]However, since when has a dissenting opinion been the _____ for persecution of faculty members on this campus? [5]_____. [6]English professors, especially, have traditionally had the reputation of fighting courageously against blockhead thinking and against lockstep decision making. [7]They have also historically been the school's champions against injustice.

[8]Their cannot be an issue closer to the basis of America's founding principles than this one because the foundation of America is based on freedom of speech. [9]The students of this university need to know whose to blame for the loss of Dr. Ruoff. [10]He is a stimulating speaker, an engaging person, and one of the finest teachers. [11]Where will this issue come to a halt? [12]Will other tenured

professors now be even more intimidated and hesitate to express any view not consistent with the general consensus of opinion? [13]Will students receive a quality education from a university that infringes on freedom of speech?

107. Which of the following words would be the best to insert into the blank in Part 4?

   (A) antagonist

   (B) catalyst

   (C) deterrent

   (D) impediment

108. Which of the following requires revision for unnecessary repetition?

   (A) Part 3

   (B) Part 6

   (C) Part 8

   (D) Part 12

109. Which of the following changes is needed in the passage above?

   (A) Part 8: Change "Their" to "There."

   (B) Part 9: Change "need" to "needs."

   (C) Part 10: Change "students" to "students'."

   (D) Part 13: Change "infringes" to "infringe."

110. Which of the following, if added between Parts 4 and 6, best supports the writer's purpose and audience?

   (A) We should allow teachers to express their own opinions regardless of what we ourselves think.

   (B) This university has always prided itself on teachers who are rather maverick in their thinking, to say the least.

   (C) Don't you think this is a pitiful way to treat a fine teacher?

   (D) One must acknowledge that university professors, as a whole, should support the opinions of fellow faculty members.

111. Which one of the following changes is needed?

    (A)   Part 8: Change "closer" to "closest."

    (B)   Part 9: Change "whose" to "who's."

    (C)   Part 10: Change "finest" to "finer."

    (D)   Part 11: Change "Where" to "When."

Read the passage below, written in the style of a student essay; then answer the four questions that follow.

[1]A growing number of businesses are providing day care facilities for the children of their employees. [2]Some companies charge a standard fee, but most provide the day care free or at a _____ cost. [3]These care programs provide services that continue through the early teens of the children. [4]Many companies are trying to decide if they should help with day care at all. [5]In the event parents need to work overtime, centers are even open on weekends, and some companies showing special initiative in building company loyalty of each employee <u>makes</u> arrangements for special field trips to zoos and museums. [6]Is this kind of care really necessary? [7]Should businesses really be in the business of day care?

[8]Experts in the field cite many advantages for this system. [9]Therefore, loyalty to the company is built, so morale climbs. [10]Studies show that when a company helps its employees blend parent and worker roles, absenteeism and tardiness drop. [11]In addition, workers feel the company has taken more of a personal interest in them. [12]Turnover becomes a much less significant factor for managers. [13]Human resource managers also estimate that every $1 spent on these programs returns $2 or more in increased productivity.

112. Which of the following improves the first paragraph?

    (A)   Change the conjunction from "but" to "and" in Part 2.

    (B)   Delete the phrase "in the event parents need to work overtime" from Part 5.

    (C)   Delete Part 4.

    (D)   Change Part 6 from an interrogative to a declarative sentence, as in "This kind of care is . . ."

113. Which of the following words would be the best to insert into the blank in Part 2?

(A) nominal

(B) astronomical

(C) exorbitant

(D) excessive

114. Which of the following should be substituted for the underlined word in Part 5?

(A) make

(B) is making

(C) should make

(D) making

115. Which of the following improves the sequence of ideas in the second paragraph?

(A) Reverse the order of Parts 8 and 9.

(B) Place Part 12 before Part 9.

(C) Delete Part 13.

(D) Place Part 9 after Part 11.

Read the passage below, written in the style of a sociology textbook; then answer the five questions that follow.

[1]A significant development during the Paleolithic period was the emergence of modern man. [2]During this time, one million years ago to 12,000 B.C., man's brain became much larger. [3]There are two suggested reasons for the rapid _____ development of man's brain. [4]First, meat eating led to big-game hunting, an activity that necessitated group planning and cooperation; and second, the use of speech to facilitate planning and coordination of group activities. [5]Tool making was once thought to be a major factor in the development of a large brain for man, but it is now known that many animals use tools and even make tools. [6]Otters will balance a rock on their stomachs as an anvil for breaking open mollusks.

[7]There are two other factors which have greatly influenced the emerging of modern man. [8]Also, food supplies increased significantly after the retreat of the great glaciers about 12,000 years ago. [9]It seems that about 100,000 years ago, genetic evolution became less important than cultural evolution as man developed the ability to pass on accumulated knowledge. [10]This increase in food supplies

may have contributed to the ability of man to increase his own numbers, thus ensuring the survival of his species.

116. Which of the following would help the focus of the main idea in the first paragraph?

    (A)   Delete Part 1.

    (B)   Reverse the order of Parts 1 and 2.

    (C)   Add a sentence after Part 2 describing the measurements and configurations of brains.

    (D)   Delete Part 6.

117. Which of the following words would be the best to insert into the blank in Part 3?

    (A)   elucidating

    (B)   elocutionary

    (C)   electrifying

    (D)   evolutionary

118. Which of the following changes is needed in the passage above?

    (A)   Part 2: Change "much" to "more."

    (B)   Part 5: Change "was" to "were."

    (C)   Part 7: Change "emerging" to "emergence."

    (D)   Part 9: Change "than" to "then."

119. Which of the following makes the sequence of ideas clearer in the second paragraph?

    (A)   Delete Part 7.

    (B)   Reverse the order of Parts 7 and 8.

    (C)   Reverse the order of Parts 8 and 9.

    (D)   Delete Part 10.

120. Which one of the following is needed?

    (A)   Part 4: Change "to facilitate" to "facilitated."

    (B)   Part 7: Delete "other."

    (C)   Part 9: Change "less" to "least."

    (D)   Part 10: Change "ensuring" to "ensured."

MATHEMATICS DEFINITIONS AND FORMULAS

Definitions

=	is equal to	≤	is less than or equal to	$\overline{AB}$	line segment AB
≠	is not equal to	π	≈ 3.14	$\overrightarrow{AB}$	line AB
>	is greater than	∠	angle	AB	length of $\overline{AB}$
<	is less than	⦜	right angle	$\dfrac{a}{b}$ or $a : b$	ratio of a to b
≥	is greater than or equal to				

Abbreviations for Units of Measurement

U.S. Customary

Distance
in. inch
ft. foot
mi. mile

Volume
gal. gallon
qt. quart
oz. fluid ounce

Weight
lb. pound
oz. ounce

Temerature °F degree Fahrenheit

Speed mph miles per hour

Metric System

Distance
m meter
km kilometer
cm centimeter
mm millimeter

Volume
L lier
mL milliliter
cc cubic centimeter

Mass
g gram
kg kilogram
mg milligram

Temperature °C degree Celsius
K Kelvin

Time
sec. second
min. minute
hr. hour

Conversions for Units of Measurement

U.S. Customary

Length
12 inches = 1 foot
3 feet = 1 yard
5280 feet = 1 mile

Volume (liquid)
8 ounces = 1 cup

2 cups = 1 pint
2 pints = 1 quart
4 quarts = 1 gallon

Weight
16 ounces = 1 pound
2000 pounds = 1 ton

Metric System

Length
10 millimeters = 1 centimeter
100 centimeters = 1 meter
1000 meters = 1 kilometer

Volume
1000 milliliters = 1 liter

1000 liters = 1 kiloliter

Weight
1000 milligrams = 1 gram
1000 grams = 1 kilogram

Square

Area = s^2
Perimeter = $4s$

Circle

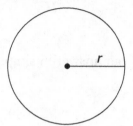

Area = πr^2
Circumference = $2\pi r$
Diameter = $2r$

Sphere

Surface area = $4\pi r^2$
Volume = $\dfrac{4}{3}\pi r^3$

Rectangle

Area = ℓw
Perimeter = $2\ell + 2w$

Cube

Surface area = $6s^2$
Volume = s^3

Rectangle

Area = $\dfrac{1}{2}bh$

Rectangular solid

Surface area = $2\ell w + 2\ell h + 2wh$
Volume = ℓwh

Right triangle

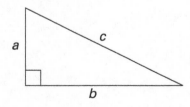

Pythagorean formula: $c^2 = a^2 + b^2$

Right circular cylinder

Surface area = $2\pi rh + 2\pi r^2$
Volume = $\pi r^2 h$

MATHEMATICS

121. Multiply $\frac{3}{4}$ by $\frac{2}{3}$. Show your answer in simplified (reduced) form.

    (A) $\frac{5}{7}$

    (B) $\frac{5}{12}$

    (C) $\frac{1}{2}$

    (D) $\frac{6}{12}$

122. Divide 6.2 by 0.05.

    (A) 124

    (B) 1.24

    (C) 12.4

    (D) 0.124

123. Perform the indicated operation:

$$(-36) - 11$$

    (A) 47

    (B) 25

    (C) −47

    (D) −25

124. Simplify: $6 \times 2 + \frac{3}{3}$

    (A) 18

    (B) 5

    (C) 10

    (D) 13

125. The number 14 is approximately 22% of which of the following numbers?

   (A) 64

   (B) 1.6

   (C) 308

   (D) 636

126. Simplify to a single term in scientific notation:

   $$(2 \times 10^3) \times (6 \times 10^4)$$

   (A) 12×10^7

   (B) 1.2×10^{12}

   (C) 1.2×10^8

   (D) 12×10^{12}

127. Bob gets $6 an hour for babysitting. His sister Keyva gets $7 an hour. One evening Bob babysat for three hours, while Keyva sat for twice that long. How much money did they take in altogether for the evening?

   (A) $60

   (B) $54

   (C) $39

   (D) $108

128. The daily high temperatures in Frostbite, Minnesota, for one week in January were as follows:

Sunday:	−2°F
Monday:	3°F
Tuesday:	0°F
Wednesday:	−4°F
Thursday:	−5°F
Friday:	−1°F
Saturday:	2°F

What was the mean daily high temperature for that week?

(A) 7

(B) −7

(C) −1

(D) 1

129. Nelson's Menswear Shop was selling sweaters for $40 at the beginning of the year. In March, the price of the sweaters was raised by 10%. In September, the price was again raised by an additional 15%. Ignoring tax, what was the price of the sweaters in September?

(A) $50.00

(B) $65.40

(C) $59.00

(D) $50.60

130. Three pounds of cherries cost $4.65. What would five pounds cost (at the same price per pound)?

(A) $7.75

(B) $7.50

(C) $23.00

(D) $23.25

131. The population of the city of Burnsville increased by approximately 0.2% last year. If the population at the beginning of the year was 1,620, what was the approximate population at the end of the year?

(A) 1,632

(B) 1,623

(C) 1,652

(D) 1,640

132. Use the pie chart below to answer the question that follows.

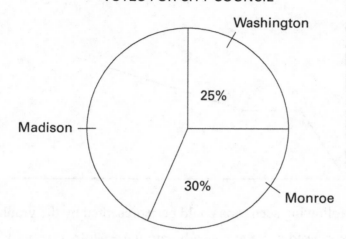

VOTES FOR CITY COUNCIL

If the total number of people voting was 600, which of the following statements are true?

    I. Madison received more votes than Monroe and Washington combined.

    II. Madison received 45% of the votes.

    III. Monroe received 180 votes.

    IV. Madison received 330 votes.

(A)   I and III only

(B)   I and IV only

(C)   II and III only

(D)   II and IV only

133. Use the graph to answer the question that follows.

Which of the following scenarios could be represented by the graph above?

(A) Mr. Cain mowed grass at a steady rate for a while, then took a short break, and then finished the job at a steady but slower rate.

(B) Mr. Cain mowed grass at a steady rate for a while, and then mowed at a steady slower rate, then he took a break.

(C) Mr. Cain mowed grass at a variable rate for a while, then took a short break, and then finished the job at a variable rate.

(D) Mr. Cain mowed grass at a steady rate for a while, then took a short break, and then finished the job at a steady but faster pace.

134. Use the bar graph that follows to answer the question.

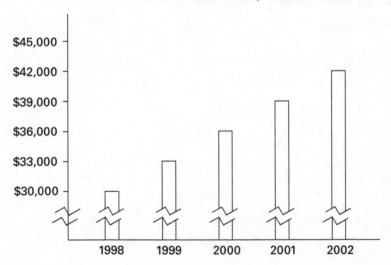

MS. PATTON'S EARNINGS, 1998–2002

Which one of the statements below is necessarily true?

(A) The range of Ms. Patton's earnings for the years shown is $15,000.

(B) Ms. Patton's annual pay increases were consistent over the years shown.

(C) Ms. Patton earned $45,000 in 2003.

(D) Ms. Patton's average income for the years shown was $38,000.

135. A line passes through points (–6, 0) and (0, 4) on the coordinate plane. Which of the following statements are true?

      I. The slope of the line is negative.

      II. The slope of the line is positive.

      III. The y-intercept of the line is –6.

      IV. The y-intercept of the line is 4.

(A) I and III only

(B) I and IV only

(C) II and III only

(D) II and IV only

136. What is the slope of a line passing through points (–2, 6) and (4, –2) on the coordinate plane?

(A) $-\dfrac{3}{4}$

(B) $\dfrac{3}{4}$

(C) $-\dfrac{4}{3}$

(D) $\dfrac{4}{3}$

137. Use the graph to answer the question.

Which equation best describes the graph above?

(A) $y = 0x$

(B) $y = x + 0$

(C) $y = -8x + 1$

(D) $y = 8x$

138. Which point represents the y-intercept of the equation $2x = 3y - 12$?

    (A) (4, 0)

    (B) (0, –6)

    (C) (–6, 0)

    (D) (0, 4)

139. Use the graph that follows to answer the question.

    Which inequality describes the graph?

    (A) $y < 3$

    (B) $x < 3$

    (C) $y > 3$

    (D) $x > 3$

140. Use the figure to answer the question that follows.

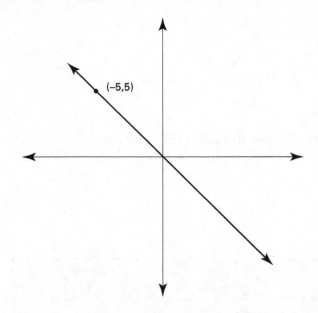

Which of the following statements about the graph of a linear equation (shown) are true?

    I.   The graph shows an inverse variation.

    II. The graph shows a direct variation.

    III. The slope of the line is −1.

    IV. The slope of the line is 1.

(A)   I and III only

(B)   I and IV only

(C)   II and III only

(D)   II and IV only

141. The following graph shows the distribution of test scores in Ms. Alvarez's class.

Which of the following statements do you know to be true?

    I.   The majority of students scored higher than 60.

    II. The test was a fair measure of ability.

    III. The mean score is probably higher than the median.

    IV. The test divided the class into distinct groups.

  (A) I and II only

  (B) I and IV only

  (C) I, III, and IV only

  (D) IV only

142. What is the solution to this equation?

$$\frac{x}{3} - 9 = 15$$

  (A) 18

  (B) 8

  (C) 36

  (D) 72

143. What are the solutions of this equation?

$$3x^2 - 11 = 1$$

  (A) 2 and –2

  (B) 3 and –3

  (C) 4 and –4

  (D) 1 and –1

144. Solve for y.

$$\frac{y}{3} - \frac{x}{2} = 4$$

(A) $y = \dfrac{3x}{2} + 12$

(B) $y = -\dfrac{3x}{2} + 12$

(C) $y = \dfrac{3x}{2} - 12$

(D) $y = -\dfrac{3x}{2} - 12$

145. Translate this problem into a one-variable equation, then solve the equation. What is the solution?

> "There are ten vehicles parked in a parking lot. Each is either a car with four tires or a motorcycle with two tires. (Do not count any spare tires.) There are 26 wheels in the lot. How many cars are there in the lot?"

(A) 8

(B) 6

(C) 5

(D) 3

146. Which equation could be used to solve the following problem?

> "Three consecutive odd numbers add up to 117. What are they?"

(A) $x + (x + 2) + (x + 4) = 117$

(B) $1x + 3x + 5x = 117$

(C) $x + x + x = 117$

(D) $x + (x + 1) + (x + 3) = 117$

147. Which equation could be used to solve the following problem?

"Here is how the Acme Taxicab Company computes fares for riders: People are charged three dollars for just getting into the cab, then they are charged two dollars more for every mile or fraction of a mile of the ride. What would be the fare for a ride of 10.2 miles?"

(A) $3 \times (2 \times 10.2) = y$

(B) $3 + (2 + 11) = y$

(C) $3 \times (2 + 10.2) = y$

(D) $3 + (2 \times 11) = y$

148. Belinda was in the woods and noticed that all the birds she saw were able to fly. She concluded that all birds could fly.

Which of the following statements about Belinda's conclusion are true?

   I. Belinda is correct in her conclusion.

   II. Belinda is incorrect in her conclusion.

   III. Belinda used inductive reasoning to reach her conclusion.

   IV. Belinda used deductive reasoning to reach her conclusion.

(A) I and III only

(B) I and IV only

(C) II and III only

(D) II and IV only

149. On day 1, Juan placed a penny in his empty piggy bank. The next day he placed two pennies in his piggy bank. On the third day, Juan placed 4 pennies in his piggy bank. If he continued this pattern, how many pennies would Juan place in his piggy bank on the tenth day?

(A) 11

(B) 16

(C) 512

(D) 256

150. There is a box of 1000 gumballs. You want to find out how many of them are yellow. You take a handful of 25 gumballs and find out there are 7 yellow gumballs in your handful. Estimate how many yellow gumballs are in the whole box.

(A) 280

(B) 357

(C) 142

(D) 400

151. The following graph represents the profits from a company over the first six months of the year.

SEMI-ANNUAL FINANCIAL REPORT (2014)

Which of the following statements are true?

    I.   There is a negative correlation between the months and profits.

    II. There is a positive correlation between the months and profits.

    III. Profits for July should be $25,000.

    IV. Profits for July should be $33,000.

(A) I and III only

(B) I and IV only

(C) II and III only

(D) II and IV only

152. When rolling two dice, what is the probability that the sum will be a multiple of 5?

    (A) $\dfrac{7}{36}$

    (B) $\dfrac{5}{36}$

    (C) $\dfrac{1}{5}$

    (D) $\dfrac{10}{36}$

153. You have a bag with 3 yellow crayons, 2 blue crayons, and 3 green crayons. What is the probability that you will draw a green crayon and flip a heads on a coin toss?

    (A) $\dfrac{3}{8}$

    (B) $\dfrac{6}{16}$

    (C) $\dfrac{3}{16}$

    (D) $\dfrac{7}{8}$

154. From the following Venn diagram, determine the probability of a child having a dog and cat at home.

PETS AT HOME

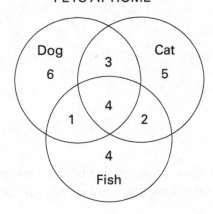

(A) $\dfrac{3}{25}$

(B) $\dfrac{7}{25}$

(C) $\dfrac{7}{21}$

(D) $\dfrac{3}{21}$

155. In the following chart, determine what type of distribution is shown.

(A) Uneven distribution

(B) Symmetric (bell-curved) distribution

(C) Left-skewed distribution

(D) Right-skewed distribution

156. Use the figure below to answer the question that follows. Assume that:

Point C is the center of the circle.

Angles xyz and xcz intercept minor arc xz.

The measure of angle xyz is 40°.

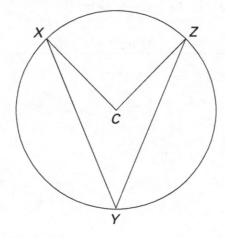

What is the measure of major arc xyz?

(A) 140°

(B) 280°

(C) 160°

(D) 320°

157. What is the approximate volume of the following cylinder?

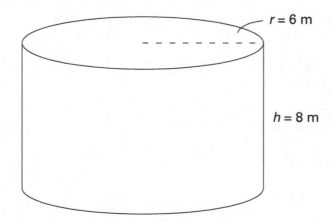

(A) 904 cm³

(B) 301 cm³

(C) 151 cm³

(D) 452 cm³

158. Use the Pythagorean theorem to answer this question: Which answer comes closest to the actual length of side *x* in the triangle below?

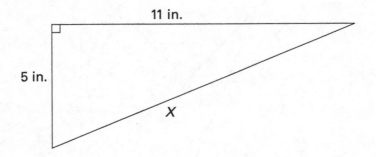

(A) 14 in.

(B) 12 in.

(C) 11 in.

(D) 13 in.

159. Sam wants to paint one of her bedroom walls. Her wall is 12 feet long and 8 feet tall. She has a window in the middle of the room that is 3 feet by 5 feet. If paint costs $1.50 per square yard, how much will it cost Sam to paint her wall?

(A) $13.50

(B) $121.50

(C) $16.00

(D) $144.00

160. Use the figure given to answer the question that follows.

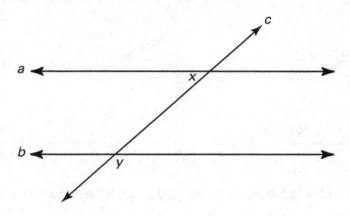

Given:
1. Lines *a* and *b* are parallel,
2. *c* is a line, and
3. the measure of angle *x* is 50°.

What is the measure of angle *y*?

(A) 50°

(B) 100°

(C) 130°

(D) 80°

161. Use the figure given to answer the question that follows. Assume that AD is a line.

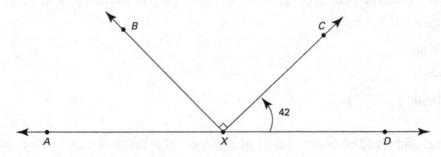

What is the measure of angle AXB?

(A) 48°

(B) 90°

(C) 42°

(D) There is not enough information to answer the question.

162. Use the figures to answer the question that follows.

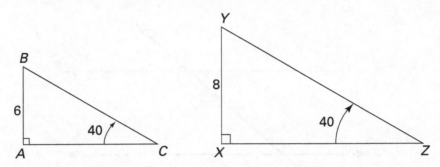

Which of the following statements about the two triangles are true?

    I.   The triangles are similar.

    II.   The triangles are congruent.

    III.   The measures of angles ABC and XYZ are the same.

    IV.   The lengths of sides BC and YZ are the same.

(A) I and III only

(B) I and IV only

(C) II and III only

(D) II and IV only

163. In a foot race, Fred beat Matt, Curt beat Dwayne, both Pat and Matt beat Ivan, Pat beat Curt, and Dwayne beat Fred. If those were the only boys racing, who came in last?

(A) Don

(B) Matt

(C) Curt

(D) Ivan

164. Kim has eight and one-third yards of material. If it takes one and two-thirds yards to make a curtain, about how many curtains can she make?

(A) 4

(B) 7

(C) 5

(D) 14

Use the following graph to answer questions 165 and 166.

Candy Color

Green	▲ ▲ ▲
Yellow	▲ ▲ ▲ ▲ ▲ ▲
Red	▲ ▲ ▲ ▲ ▲ ▲ ▲ ▲ ▲
Blue	▲ ▲ ▲ ▲ ▲ ▲
Orange	▲ ▲ ▲ ▲

▲ = ? candies

165. This graph represents which type of data?

   (A)   Continuous

   (B)   Discrete

   (C)   Normally Distributed

   (D)   Skewed

166. If the key was not given and you knew there were 12 green candies, how many red candies do you have?

   (A)   9

   (B)   27

   (C)   4

   (D)   36

167. The local manufacturer needs to figure out how much paper it will take to create a label that will wrap around its newly-designed jar of jam. If the picture below represents the jar, estimate how many square inches of paper will be needed.

$r = 3$ cm

(A) $45\pi\,\text{cm}^2$

(B) $90\pi\,\text{cm}^2$

(C) $99\pi\,\text{cm}^2$

(D) $108\pi\,\text{cm}^2$

168. Given that you start, on day one, with a 6-square-inch patch of mold and that it doubles each day, which formula would be the formula you would use to determine the square inches of mold after "n" number of days?

(A) $y = 6(2^n)$

(B) $y = 6(2^{n-1})$

(C) $y = 2(6^{n-1})$

(D) $y = 2(6^n)$

169. Bryson wants to hang 5 shelves that are 23 and three-fourths inches long. Approximately, how many linear feet of wood does he need to buy?

(A) 58 feet

(B) 33 feet

(C) 116 feet

(D) 10 feet

170. Solve for y.

$$2x - 3y = 6$$

(A) $y = \dfrac{3}{2}x - 3$

(B) $y = -\dfrac{3}{2}x + 3$

(C) $y = \dfrac{2}{3}x - 2$

(D) $y = -\dfrac{2}{3}x + 2$

WRITING ASSIGNMENT

Read the passage below on studying literature of the past, and then follow the instructions for writing your essay.

Many scholars note the decline of interest in literature written before the twentieth century. A diminishing number of students pursue studies in Classical, Medieval, and even Renaissance literature. Some observers think this trend is acceptable, since the literature of these early periods is not particularly interesting to the general public. Others say that any lessening of study about the past, and especially its artistic expression, is a negative trend.

In an essay written to an English teacher, argue whether you feel that the trend of studying modern versus past literature is commendable or contemptible. Reflect on modern culture and the effects of literature upon it. Discuss the advantages and/or disadvantages of a course of study that excludes or minimizes the literature of earlier periods. Finally, draw upon your own exposure to and attitude toward modern and past literatures, respectively.

You may write in the space provided.

ANSWER KEY FOR PRACTICE TEST

1. (B)	23. (A)	45. (B)	67. (C)
2. (A)	24. (B)	46. (C)	68. (D)
3. (C)	25. (A)	47. (B)	69. (D)
4. (D)	26. (B)	48. (B)	70. (C)
5. (D)	27. (C)	49. (C)	71. (D)
6. (B)	28. (C)	50. (B)	72. (B)
7. (A)	29. (B)	51. (D)	73. (A)
8. (C)	30. (D)	52. (D)	74. (C)
9. (C)	31. (D)	53. (C)	75. (D)
10. (A)	32. (C)	54. (A)	76. (D)
11. (D)	33. (B)	55. (B)	77. (A)
12. (A)	34. (B)	56. (B)	78. (A)
13. (D)	35. (D)	57. (C)	79. (B)
14. (D)	36. (A)	58. (B)	80. (B)
15. (A)	37. (D)	59. (C)	81. (A)
16. (A)	38. (A)	60. (D)	82. (D)
17. (B)	39. (B)	61. (B)	83. (A)
18. (A)	40. (A)	62. (C)	84. (B)
19. (B)	41. (B)	63. (A)	85. (A)
20. (C)	42. (A)	64. (D)	86. (B)
21. (D)	43. (D)	65. (B)	87. (B)
22. (B)	44. (C)	66. (C)	88. (C)

ANSWER KEY (continued)

89. (B)	110. (B)	131. (B)	151. (D)
90. (B)	111. (B)	132. (C)	152. (A)
91. (C)	112. (C)	133. (A)	153. (C)
92. (A)	113. (A)	134. (B)	154. (A)
93. (B)	114. (A)	135. (D)	155. (D)
94. (A)	115. (D)	136. (C)	156. (B)
95. (C)	116. (D)	137. (C)	157. (A)
96. (A)	117. (D)	138. (D)	158. (B)
97. (B)	118. (C)	139. (A)	159. (A)
98. (C)	119. (C)	140. (C)	160. (C)
99. (B)	120. (A)	141. (B)	161. (A)
100. (D)	121. (C)	142. (D)	162. (A)
101. (D)	122. (A)	143. (A)	163. (D)
102. (D)	123. (C)	144. (A)	164. (C)
103. (B)	124. (D)	145. (D)	165. (B)
104. (C)	125. (A)	146. (A)	166. (D)
105. (C)	126. (C)	147. (D)	167. (B)
106. (C)	127. (A)	148. (C)	168. (B)
107. (B)	128. (C)	149. (C)	169. (D)
108. (C)	129. (D)	150. (A)	170. (C)
109. (A)	130. (A)		

DETAILED EXPLANATIONS FOR PRACTICE TEST

READING

1. **(B)**

    (B) is correct because sunlight and particles cause a color change in water. (A), (C), and (D) do not cause water to change its appearance of color. (Standard 3.3)

2. **(A)**

    The informational passage discusses the topic of water; therefore, the most important "source of sediment" is not a fact relevant to water and its properties. (Standard 5.2)

3. **(C)**

    (C) is the answer because "most unusual" is not a fact. It is an opinion. (A), (B), and (D) are facts stated in the passage. (Standard 5.4)

4. **(D)**

    (D) is a figure of speech because molten lava is being compared to having similar properties to water. (A), (B), and (C) are incorrect because they are not making similar comparisons to water. (Standard 2.4)

5. **(D)**

    (D) is correct because its precepts are summations of each of the composition's main paragraphs. Choice (A) only mentions points made in the second paragraph; (B) and (C) only mention scattered points made throughout the passage, each of which does not represent a larger body of information within the passage. (Standard 6.1)

6. **(B)**

    The second paragraph states that this is the reason that water is a most unusual substance. Choices (A) and (C) list unusual properties of water, but are not developed in the same manner as the property stated in (B). Choice (D) is not correct under any circumstances. (Standard 2.3)

7. **(A)**

   The sentence contrasts distilled water to that which contains salt, so (A) is correct. Choices (B), (C), and (D) are not implied by the passage. (Standard 1.1)

8. **(C)**

   The writer's didactic summary of water's properties is the only perspective found in the passage. Choices (A) and (B) are the subjects of individual paragraphs within the passage, but hardly represent the entire passage itself. An in-depth discussion of the physical states of liquids is not offered within the passage. (Standard 3.1)

9. **(C)**

   The correct choice is (C) because of the many properties of water ascribed to it in the passage, each of which might serve one practical purpose or another. Choices (A) and (D) are contradicted within the passage, while (B) is not implied at all by the passage. (Standard 3.4)

10. **(A)**

    Answer (A) is correct. *Except* and *accept* are the proper words to use in the blank spaces. (B), (C), and (D) word pairs do not provide meaning to the sentences. (Standard 1.2)

11. **(D)**

    (D) is the correct answer because the author is showing bias toward the SONAR device. (A), (B), and (C) are factual statements. (Standard 5.5)

12. **(A)**

    Choice (A) is correct because of the importance of streamlining mentioned in the final paragraph. Choices (B) and (C) are not suggested in the paragraph, and (D) is secondary in importance to (A). (Standard 3.2)

13. **(D)**

    Since it may be inferred from the general purpose of underwater detection equipment, (D) is correct. While (A) and (B) are true statements, they are not inferences. (C) is not implied in the passage. (Standard 3.4)

14. **(D)**

    Choice (D) is correct because the R in SONAR stands for "ranging." Choices (A), (B), and (C) are neither mentioned nor implied by the passage. (Standard 1.1)

15. **(A)**

    As was mentioned in the third sentence of the third paragraph, (A) is correct. Choices (B), (C), and (D) are not mentioned in the passage. It may be inferred that Bushnell's invention led to the success of the later version of the submarine. Choices (B) and (C) are true, but are not inferences because they are directly stated in the first paragraph. (D) is not a true statement; the Turtle had no direct link to the 1864 incident. (Standard 2.3)

16. **(A)**

    It may be inferred that Bushnell's invention led to the success of the later version of the submarine. Choices (B) and (C) are true, but are not inferences because they are directly stated in the first paragraph. (D) is not a true statement; the Turtle had no direct link to the 1864 incident. (Standard 4.4)

17. **(B)**

    Even though people in America opposed the idea of hiring immigrants, they hired immigrants because of the labor shortage. Therefore, (B) is the correct answer. (Standard 4.2)

18. **(A)**

    (A) is correct because it identifies similarities of results from rapid growth. (C) and (D) are incorrect. We do not know if immigrants lived peacefully and it is unknown when a state militia was created. (B) is also incorrect. According to the passage, cities could not keep up with services, much less provide good service to all of its citizens. (Standard 4.1)

19. **(B)**

    A fallacy is an error in reasoning. It cannot be assumed that everyone who travels will experience discrimination. Therefore, (B) is the correct answer. (A), (C), and (D) are factual in nature. (Standard 5.3)

20. **(C)**

    Choice (C) is correct because it traces the development of the passage with the author's perspective in mind. While (A) and (B) are mentioned in the passage, they are not overriding concerns in the passage. (D) does not directly apply to the passage. (Standard 3.1)

21. **(D)**

The correct response is (D) because the incident is situated with other acts of violent aggression. Choices (A) and (C) are not implied by the context of the mob riot situation, and (B) is not implied at all by the paragraph. (Standard 1.3)

22. **(B)**

The correct answer is (B) because it represents a theme prevalent in the fourth paragraph. Both (A) and (D) represent individual strands within the paragraph, but do not express its main idea; (C) is not mentioned or implied in the paragraph. (Standard 6.2)

23. **(A)**

All of the urban difficulties that are mentioned in the passage stem from the rapid growth of immigration. Neither (B) nor (C) is implied within the passage. Choice (D) has no direct bearing on the development of the passage. (Standard 5.1)

24. **(B)**

The combined percentages of English and German immigrants equal 45 percent (Irish immigrants represent 43 percent of the graph). Choice (A) is incorrect because the Irish immigrants represent less than half of the graph. Choice (C) is incorrect because the graph nowhere implies that the "All Others" section of the graph is restricted to Italian immigrants. (D) is incorrect because the English and German percentages are unequal. (Standard 6.3)

25. **(A)**

The last sentence in these instructions tells the student that the paper must be proofread with no "mechanical" (punctuation) errors. The third sentence states that an understanding of the reading material is required. Answers (B) and (C) contain only a portion of the needed requirements, while (D) is completely inaccurate. Thus, (A) is the correct answer. (Standard 4.4)

26. **(B)**

As used in the passage, the term "sophisticated prose" means that the student must write a readable paper using thoughtful language, thereby demonstrating a familiarity with the primary text. Answers (A), (C), and (D) all contain language that suggests the opposite of a readable paper. (Standard 1.1)

27. **(C)**

A primary text is the source material, or the main or principal text used in an assignment. The remaining answers (A), (B), and (D) refer to either secondary materials or reference sources. (Standard 1.1)

28. **(C)**

The passage suggests that education is primarily based on failure as negative reinforcement and that, in order to create a more productive and positive learning environment, the emphasis must shift to success. While answers (A) and (B) may be correct, they are not the main idea of the passage. (D) is simply a statement that is not based upon any factual evidence whatsoever. Therefore, (C) is the correct answer. (Standard 2.1)

29. **(B)**

A *maxim* in this case is another word for *motto*. It can also mean an accepted truism or principle, which would also apply here. Answers (A), (C), and (D) are erroneous definitions; therefore, (B) maxim is the correct answer. (Standard 1.1)

30. **(D)**

The passage states that "the language of failure . . . will have a prohibitive impact on the students' self-esteem;" thus, (D) is the correct answer. Answers (A), (B), and (C) do not apply in this case. (Standard 2.3)

31. **(D)**

The first paragraph of the passage tells the reader that, in addition to personal expression, language also has the power to "persuade and influence." While answers (A), (B), and (C) may indeed be attributes of language, they are not focused upon in the passage. (Standard 2.3)

32. **(C)**

The passage suggests that Douglass was concerned with raising social consciousness about slavery. His interest in refuting those who doubted his claims was for the sake of authenticity. (Standard 2.3)

33. **(B)**

Douglass was one of the eminent human rights leaders of the nineteenth century. All the other choices, while true, are irrelevant to the question and are not supported by the text. (Standard 2.1)

34. **(B)**

The passage states "Mrs. Auld recognized Frederick's intellectual acumen." (A) synonym for *acumen* is *intelligence*, *insight*, or *natural ability*. The other choices are inaccurate. (Standards 1.4, 3.4)

35. **(D)**

Choices (A), (B), and (C) are too vague or ill-defined. Thus, choice (D) is correct. (Standard 3.2)

36. **(A)**

An "impromptu" speech is one given extemporaneously, or off the cuff. (Standard 1.1)

37. **(D)**

A teaching assistant would be expected to lay the foundation for her lecture and then present greater detail by way of example, or as the passage puts it, "illustration." Someone in this position, having set this task for herself, would not be prone to refuting her own lecture notes (A), attempting to cause confusion (B), or perhaps least of all, working to subvert the lecture topic she herself had elected to teach (C). (Standard 1.1)

38. **(A)**

The definition of the term *pedagogical* is (A), academic. The answers (B) abstract, (C) meaningless, and (D) obtuse are incorrect. (Standard 1.1)

39. **(B)**

The author's classroom experience was (B), intelligible (understandable) and pragmatic (practical or utilitarian). The passage gives credence to this by the author's use of such words as "clear and well prepared." Answers (A), and (C) suggest the opposite of a positive experience, and there is no evidence given that the experience was too advanced or complicated (D). (Standard 3.4)

40. **(A)**

   The passage tells of the "great (linguistic) vowel shift" of the early fifteenth century. While the passage speaks of (B) an artistic renaissance, (C) new linguistic freedoms, and (D) effects on artistic expression, these are all results of the shift and not the shift itself. The shift is what the passage is about. Thus, (A) is the correct answer. ((Standard 2.1)

41. **(B)**

   In this case, linguistic refers to speaking, talking, verbiage, and/or the act of oration. (A), (C), and (D) are not acceptable definitions for the word *linguistic*. Consequently, Choice (B), verbal or rhetorical, is the correct answer. (Standard 1.1)

42. **(A)**

   Answers (B), (C), and (D) are generalized answers resulting from the vowel shift. Choice (A) is a direct result of the shift and is quoted directly from the passage. Therefore, (A) is the correct answer. (Standard 2.2)

43. **(D)**

   The passage states that lead poisoning leads to learning disabilities and possibly even death. Choice (A) is too broad, and (B) and (C) are not directly addressed, leaving (D) as the correct answer. (Standard 2.3)

44. **(C)**

   The passage states that "all California MediCal-eligible children, ages one through five, will now be routinely screened." Answer choices (A) children in California, (B) children with learning disabilities, and (D) minority children, are generalities not stated in the passage. Only Choice (C) is clearly stated in the passage. (Standard 2.3)

45. **(B)**

   The statistics suggest that inner-city children are at the greatest risk from lead poisoning. The statistics do not support answers (A), (C), and (D), leaving (B) as the only legitimate answer. (Standard 2.3)

46. **(C)**

   The last sentence of the passage suggests that testing will catch the disease "at an early stage" and prevent serious disorders. Choices (A), (B), and (D) do not address this ultimate goal of the testing program. Only Choice (C) reiterates the program's ultimate purpose. (Standards 3.4, 4.4)

47. **(B)**

The ranchers believe that killing the eagles will protect their ranches. This is understood by the implication that "attract[ing] and kill[ing] predators . . . in an effort to preserve young grazing animals" will protect their ranches. (Standards 3.4, 4.4)

48. **(B)**

The author's use of words such as "mighty bald eagle" and "threatened by a new menace" supports concern for the topic. For the most part, the author appears objective; thus, Choice (B), concerned interest, is the correct answer. (Standard 3.4)

49. **(C)**

The author remains objective throughout the passage. That is, he remains impartial and factual. Answer (A) *lethargy* means sluggish; (B) *apathy* means unconcerned. (D) *intensity* means vehement or fierce, and thus does not apply. (Standard 3.4)

50. **(B)**

The third sentence suggests that poetry has the ability to serve both as an adornment or embellishment of an era and as a social commentary. The passage fundamentally suggests that poetry is more than just lyrical fluff, it is a means of social analysis, protest, and interpretation. While (A), (C), and (D) are components of the passage, they are not the passage's main topic. (Standard 2.1)

51. **(D)**

The word *trope* means that a word is used in a figurative sense. That is, it conjures images of Greco-Roman representations. Answer (A) is a troop; (B) and (C) are types of terminology that do not apply. (Standard 1.3)

52. **(D)**

The writer concludes that lyric poetry can be a vehicle to express social commentary. Therefore, (D) is the correct answer. (A), (B), and (C) are not accurate conclusions for the meaning of the passage. (Standard 4.4)

53. **(C)**

    The meaning of *tempestuous* in the passage can be derived from the words *confrontations, paradoxes*, and *ironies*. Therefore, (C) is the correct answer. (A), (B), and (D) do not provide a meaning for the word from the context clues. (Standard 1.1)

54. **(A)**

    (A) is the correct answer because it provides the best implied main idea, which is the use of lyric poetry. (B), (C), and (D) do not provide the implied main idea for the passage. (Standard 3.2)

55. **(B)**

    The passage suggests that a critic is a viable political force that serves both as a censure and a social commentator. Answers (A), (C), and (D) are subjective answers and are, therefore, inappropriate. (Standard 2.1)

56. **(B)**

    The passage states that the etymology of the word *censure* dates to the Middle Ages, suggesting that it was in use at that time. The passage also states that a critic can also be equivalent to a censurer. Therefore, the correct answer could not be (A) a modern phenomenon, or (D) developed around the time of the Civil War. Answer (C) is not addressed in the passage, leaving (B) as the best answer. (Standard 2.3)

57. **(C)**

    The passage addresses both the implications (indications) and the connotations (meaning) associated with the role of the critic as author. Answers (B) and (D) are only alluded to, while (A) is a supposition. Thus, (C) is the correct answer. (Standard 3.2)

58. **(B)**

    Etymology is the study of the history and/or origin of a word. This definition renders the remaining answers false. (Standard 1.1)

59. **(C)**

    The correct answer is (C), which states that critics understand the delicate balance inherent in their professional role. Answer (A) is a false statement, since critics are not always supportive and positive about a writer's work. There is no mention of the critic's role as being an efficient approach to providing criticism, so (D) is incorrect. Critics may sometimes be arrogant and reflect an "air of superiority," but the statement does not summarize the passage; therefore (B) is an incorrect answer. (Standard 6.2)

60. **(D)**

The author of the passage is trying to persuade the reader to believe that a critic as a censurer is viewed as a negative person who exerts his own opinions on literary art, therefore, (D) is the correct answer. (A), (B), and (C) are incorrect as the passage does not state that reviews are fair, impartial, objective, and representative of public opinion. (Standard 3.1)

LANGUAGE ARTS

61. **(B)**

The presence of "the" before "Westown's" means that the reference is to the council, not to a council belonging to Westown. The other choices are all currently correct, and changing them would make them nonstandard. (Standards 7.1, 7.3, 8.1)

62. **(C)**

The word *decisive* means that the votes served to decide the outcome. The other choices cast doubt on the role of the three votes in the final tally. (Standards 7.3, 11.1, 11.3)

63. **(A)**

The editorial is suggesting that the population loss is a bad thing and that proposed changes would be a good thing. Thus, population loss is something the author wants stopped, or at least lessened, so *alleviate*, which means "to lessen" is the only possible choice. (Standard 7.1)

64. **(D)**

The subject of the first clause is "each," which is singular, so the verb should be "has." (Standard 7.1)

65. **(B)**

Choice (A) is wrong because it makes no sense within the sentence; the zoning regulations cannot be easy to change. Choice (C) makes sense, but its use of "them" is ambiguous—does it refer to the authors or the regulations? Choice (D) is wrong because, if the authors said the regulations would be hard to change, the word *apparently* earlier in the sentence would make no sense. Thus, Choice (B) is the best answer. (Standards 7.1, 7.2, 7.3, 11.1, 11.4)

66. **(C)**

This sentence includes a remark about the "lack of spark" in (C) DeMarco's writing, which makes a contrast with the previous sentence, where his potential reading competence is regarded as positive. The rest of the paragraph supports this observation. Choice (B) is also supported by the rest of the paragraph, but it contains no transition of contrast (*moreover* rather than *however*). (Standards 12.1, 12.2, 12.5)

67. **(C)**

The best answer here is Part 6, with its "grasps and comprehends." These two words mean exactly the same thing in this context, so one of them is unnecessary. The phrase "all of the class" in Part 3 is somewhat wordy (it could be "the whole class"), but it is not redundant. (Standards 12.4)

68. **(D)**

Part 13 contains a dangling modifier. The verbal phrase at the beginning of the sentence should modify a person ("answers" cannot be asked a question), but the only choices are "his" and "answers." Thus the phrase modifies nothing and is a dangling modifier. (Standards 12.2, 12.3)

69. **(D)**

The sentence in Part 12 refers to journals of all classmates, so the apostrophe should follow the *s*. Choice (A) is wrong because *Sideways Stories from Wayside School* is a book, not a story, a fact that prospective elementary teachers should know. If you didn't, you should get to know some of the more popular authors for elementary school. (Standards 7.1, 8.1, 8.3)

70. **(C)**

The phrase "comings and goings" could possibly fit into this sentence, but it is slightly off, whereas the other choices have little or nothing wrong with them. One problem with "comings and goings" is its informal tone: a case study in a textbook usually does not use slangy terms like this one. In addition, the sentence refers to all the students' accounts, not just their travels. (Standard 11.4)

71. **(D)**

The preceding sentence provides a context for the type of answers provided, i.e., "his writing lacks detail." As a result, the only option that is consistent with his earlier written account is that his answers were "evasive." (Standards 7.3, 11.3, 11.4)

72. **(B)**

The sentence in Part 6 begins with "Although"—used for mentioning the scientists' public statements—and refers to the "hazy" benefits derived from the study. Thus the sentence has to deal with speculation about the "uncertain" benefits. Choice (D) fits in with the paragraph's development fairly well, but it not the best answer because the pejorative word "racist" would not generally be used to characterize someone in a textbook. (There is little doubt that the author considers the experiment itself to be racist, but he or she does not otherwise characterize any of the individuals involved in this passage—and should not do so without offering evidence.) (Standards 9.1, 9.2)

73. **(A)**

The word should be *affected*; see the discussion of *effect* and *affect* in Chapter 2. The other words are used in standard ways and, even though *whereas* may sound out of place, it is not as obviously wrong as *effected* and therefore is not the best answer. (Standard 11.4)

74. **(C)**

Part 7 contains a comma splice. The sentence has two independent clauses, and they are not joined by a coordinating conjunction. They must therefore be separated by a semicolon, not a comma. Part 3, which contains several commas, is correctly punctuated (except for the period at the end), but they are all necessary to separate the two nonrestrictive phrases: (a) *author of the excellent history on the subject* and (b) *Bad Blood*. (Standard 8.1)

75. **(D)**

By convention in American English, periods and commas are always placed inside quotation marks. (Standards 7.1, 7.3, 8.1)

76. **(D)**

The verb *learn* should clearly be in the past tense, not present, because it concerns something that happened in 1972. Incidentally, the word *media* is technically plural, so the verb form should be *learn* rather than *learns* even if present tense were correct. (Standard 7.1)

77. **(A)**

The verb *touted* is the only choice that clearly describes the manner in which the scientists announced the "great scientific merits" of the study. (Standards 7.1, 11.1, 11.3)

78. **(A)**

The last phrase of the sentence—"that chaotic period"—could refer to either the guerilla war mentioned in Part 12 or the period of relocation mentioned in Part 13, meaning that the sentence would have to be inserted after Part 12 or 13 (choices (A) or (B)). However, the sentence about the Church's individual members providing support cannot just sit beside a sentence about the Church itself providing support: the two thoughts would have to be joined in a logical way. Thus choice (B) is not as good as choice (A). With choice (A), Part 12 would be explained by the new sentence, and then Part 13 would describe the circumstances under which the support was provided. (Standards 11.2, 12.1)

79. **(B)**

The second paragraph proceeds from the 1500s to 1975, and the third paragraph describes the cause for the effect mentioned at the end of the second paragraph: the embrace of Catholicism by the Timorese. (Standards 10.1, 10.2, 10.3)

80. **(B)**

Part 4 is a sentence fragment: because *being* is a verbal rather than a standard verb form, it does not act as a verb for *exceptions*. (Note: Substituting *were* for *being* would fix the fragment but would not produce an effective sentence—"the exceptions" to what?) Part 7 does contain a punctuation error, but the question specifically asks for nonstandard "sentence structure." Be sure to read each question thoroughly. (Standard 12.5)

81. **(A)**

Part 7 begins with a subordinate clause, and a comma should separate that clause from the independent clause that follows. The *who* in Part 8 is correct even though it refers to "missionaries," which is the object of a preposition, because it is the subject of its own clause—"who were posted." The *its* following East Timor in Part 9 is correct because the pronoun refers to the country as a whole, not to all the people of the country. The word *government* in Part 11 is not capitalized even though it occurs with the proper adjective "Indonesian." (Standards 7.2, 8.1, 8.2)

82. **(D)**

Because the first blank must show a contrast with the previous thought, choice (B) is not possible. Because a comma rather than a semicolon precedes the first blank, *however* is not possible, either. If *however* were inserted, the sentence would have a comma splice, because *however* is not a coordinating conjunction (*but* is). (Standard 11.5)

83. **(A)**

The first sentence has a plural subject—"animism and spirit worship"—so it should have a plural form of verb as well. (Standard 7.1)

84. **(B)**

Among the four adjectives that constitute the options, the only one that accurately describes the "misery of the people" is "abject." The other three options are either positive or neutral in their characterization, which is inconsistent with the condition of the people. (Standards 7.3, 11.3, 11.4)

85. **(A)**

In Part 1 the singular noun *Lincoln Cent* requires use of the singular verb *was*. (Standards 7.1, 7.2)

86. **(B)**

The adjectival form *second*, not the adverbial form *secondly*, is appropriate here, since it modifies a noun, not a verb. (Standard 7.3)

87. **(B)**

The opening verbal phrase is a dangling modifier. "Prevention" is not "faced" with anything; Lincoln is. All the other choices are standard English sentences. (Standards 7.1, 8.3, 11.3)

88. **(C)**

"With the outbreak . . ." is a prepositional phrase that is stopped with a period[.]. It has no subject or verb and is not a standard English sentence. All the rest are correct English. (Standards 12.3, 12.4, 12.5)

89. **(B)**

    The sentence requires the past participle of *bear*, which is *borne*. The other options are inconsistent with the context of the sentence, which honors the sacrifices of the men who fought in battle. (Standards 7.1, 11.3, 11.4)

90. **(B)**

    In (B) the comma is not necessary since the sentence does not contain an independent or dependent clause. The phrase "at one time . . ." in (A) is a nonrestrictive unit that is not necessary to the basic meaning of the sentence; consequently, both commas are needed. The comma for (D) is necessary to set off a qualifying phrase. No commas are needed in (C) since the phrase that follows is a direct adjectival qualification of what kind of rockets they are as we know them today. Thus, no comma of separation is needed. (Standard 8.1)

91. **(C)**

    The principle posited by Goddard is part of his overall theory; therefore, *theoretically* is the appropriate option. (Standards 7.3, 11.1, 11.3)

92. **(A)**

    In Part 5 the *experiments* took place during the early part of the decade. As a result, use of the possessive *1920's* is not appropriate and should be changed to the *1920s*. (Standards 7.1, 7.3, 7.4)

93. **(B)**

    This is just a long phrase; it has no subject or verb. (C) is an atypical, but rhetorically correct and a standard English sentence. Many sentences in English begin with *And*. The other choices are standard subject/verb independent sentence units. (Standards 12.3, 12.4, 12.5)

94. **(A)**

    The word *thing* is too general for such a specific informational context. (B) should remain because it is the exact, or first, phrase the writer discusses. (C) need not be changed because only a synonym such as *real* would be needed, but the meaning would remain the same. (D) is correct because the writer points not to any specific study, research, or development done, but to all that type of "work" in general. (Standard 11.4)

95. **(C)**

It is not the work force that is "for the better," but the situation for men. This is also supported by the rest of the evidence offered in the paragraph. The other sentences have their modifying phrases directly related to the idea they qualify. (Standard 11.4)

96. **(A)**

The sentence refers to one who benefits from the "increasing presence of women in the workplace." As a result, the only two possible options are *benefactor* and *beneficiary*. Given *benefactor* refers to one who confers a benefit and *beneficiary* refers to one who receives a benefit, the latter is the correct noun to use in this sentence. (Standards 11.1, 11.3, 11.4)

97. **(B)**

The writer is comparing before and after the appearance of women in management—only two things—therefore the comparative form, not the superlative, is correct: *greater*. (A), (C), and (D) are all incorrect responses; they have no comparative adjectives, just adverbs used as qualifiers, e.g., "overly." These are used in a standard way. (Standards 10.1, 10.2, 10.3, 12.1)

98. **(C)**

In Part 14, given that *women* is the plural of *woman*, it would be grammatically incorrect to use *womens* to pluralize a word that is already the plural of the original word. In addition, the sentence requires use of the possessive plural noun *women's*. (Standards 7.1, 7.4, 11.3)

99. **(B)**

Part 15 is a run-on sentence, incorrectly punctuated with a comma after "families" instead of a period or a semicolon (i.e., it's a comma splice). The rest of the choices are all standard sentences. (Standards 12.3, 12.4, 12.5)

100. **(D)**

Part 12 has an incorrect agreement between "kids" and "does." *Kids* [they] *do* [something] is correct. All the other sentences use standard English syntax. (Standard 7.1)

101. **(D)**

The sentence requires an adverb that modifies the verb *creating*. The definition of *imagination* includes *creative ability*, which is consistent with the use of the adverb *imaginatively* in this context. (Standards 7.3, 11.2, 11.3)

102. **(D)**

The sentence is a rhetorical clause that begins with a subordinating conjunction, *because*. Consequently, it cannot stand alone as a complete standard sentence. The rest are standard. (Standards 12.3, 12.4, 12.5)

103. **(B)**

The writer never specifies with the correct noun who exactly is placing the baby in her jumpseat. None of the other choices is a required correction. (Standards 7.1, 7.2, 7.3)

104. **(C)**

Choice (C) is a prepositional phrase, "About 25,000 years ago," which is followed by a subordinate clause. This part should be linked to the previous sentence as it is integral to the migration of the Anasazi. Choices (A), (B), and (D) are all complete sentences. (Standards 12.3, 12.4, 12.5)

105. **(C)**

The passage chronicles the history of the Anasazi. This sentence serves to describe the culmination or height of the Anasazi's achievements. The noun *zenith* is defined as a "culminating point" and would be the only appropriate choice. (Standards 11.1, 11.3, 11.4)

106. **(C)**

Choice (C) has to do with the later history of the Mesa Verde area, after the Anasazi had abandoned it. Since this is so far removed chronologically, Part 7 should be deleted or further developed in a third paragraph. Choices (A) and (B) discuss the very early history of the Anasazi. Choice (D) follows the chronological time order from A.D. 500 and leads into a discussion of the height of the Anasazi civilization. (Standards 10.1, 10.2, 10.3, 10.5, 12.2)

107. **(B)**

The sentence requires a noun that reflects a causal relationship; specifically one that defines the possible result of "dissenting opinions" in bringing about "persecution of a faculty member." The noun *catalyst* is defined as an "agent that provokes change or action" and would be the only appropriate choice among the four options. (Standards 7.3, 11.3, 11.4)

108. **(C)**

Choice (C) unnecessarily repeats the words *basis, based, founding*, and *foundation*. These forms need not be repeated and the sentence should be condensed. Choice (A) repeats the phrase *board of regents*, found in the previous sentence, but it is needed for transition of thought. Choice (B) and choice (D) are well-worded sentences. (Standards 10.1, 10.4, 12.4)

109. **(A)**

In Part 8 the third person plural possessive adjective "Their" is mistakenly used and should be substituted with "There," the appropriate pronoun that introduces a noun or clause. (Standards 7.1, 7.2, 8.1)

110. **(B)**

Choice (B) fits between Part 4 and Part 6. Part 4 mentions the topic of dissenting opinion, and Part 6 elaborates by stating the position that English professors have always been outspoken. This idea is continued in Part 7. Choice (A) changes voice to "we," which is out of place in this letter. Choice (C) is too casual. Choice (D) directly contradicts the thesis of the letter. (Standards 9.1, 9.2, 9.3, 9.4)

111. **(B)**

Choice (B) contains an inappropriate use of words. The contraction for *who is* should be used to make the sentence correct. The possessive *whose* is not correct in this context. Choice (A) correctly uses the comparative degree. Choice (C) correctly uses the superlative degree. Choice (D) does not make a needed change. (Standards 7.1, 7.2, 7.3)

112. **(C)**

Choice C, delete Part 4, is the correct choice. The sentence labeled Part 4 introduces a new topic—the fact that some companies are not committed to a day care program. Since the paragraphs are both discussing companies that have already made this decision, and the advantages of having made this decision, Part 4 is out of place. Choice (A) would make a contradictory statement. Choice (B) would delete a needed phrase. Choice (D) would destroy the parallelism created with Parts 6 and 7 that leads naturally as a transition into the next paragraph. (Standards 11.1, 11.2, 11.3, 11.4, 11.5, 12.1, 12.5)

113. **(A)**

Three of the options—choices (B), (C), and (D)—are adjectives used to describe or define situations that exceed "customary or appropriate limits." The sentence, however, requires an adjective that serves to describe or define a day care fee within a range from "free" to "standard." As a result, "nominal" would be the appropriate adjective to use in this situation. (Standards 7.3, 11.3, 11.4)

114. **(A)**

Choice (A) is needed for correct subject and verb agreement. The plural subject *companies* should be followed by the plural verb *make*. Confusion is caused by an intervening phrase, "showing special initiative in building company loyalty of each employee." Because the phrase ends with a singular noun, it is a common error to make the verb singular also. Choice (B), present progressive, and choice C, future, are incorrect tenses for the context of the sentence and the paragraph. Choice (D) needs a helping verb and cannot stand alone. (Standards 11.3)

115. **(D)**

Part 9 begins with the transition word *Therefore*, so it is best placed after a sentence that would state a reason for building company loyalty and morale. Part 11 gives a compelling reason—the company's personal interest in each employee. Choice (A) would remove the topic sentence to a less prominent position, as well as have Part 9 clearly out of order with no idea before it in the paragraph. Choice (B) does not place a sentence with a clear reason before the transition *therefore*. Choice (C) would weaken the paragraph. (Standards 11.2, 11.4, 12.1)

116. **(D)**

Choice (D) discusses the tool-making abilities of an otter, not man, so it should be deleted. Choice (A) would delete the topic sentence from the paragraph. Choice (B) is incorrect because Part 2 begins with "During this time," and there would be no antecedent for "this" if the two parts were reversed. Choice (C) is incorrect because the suggested addition does not pertain to the development of man during this time period. (Standards 10.2, 10.5, 11.1)

117. **(D)**

The sentence in Part 3 requires an adjective that modifies the noun *development* within a context that serves to further define the "significant development" of the Paleolithic period. As a result, the only adjective among the options that is appropriate would be *evolutionary*. (Standards 7.3, 11.1, 11.3)

118. **(C)**

In Part 7 the sentence requires the use of a noun, not a verb, specifically, the noun *emergence*, which is used to define the "act or instance of emerging," not the actual intransitive verb *emerging*. (Standards 7.1, 7.3)

119. (C)

Parts 8 and 9 need to be reversed. Part 8 begins with the transition word *Also*, which clearly introduces a second feature, not a first, as the position would indicate. Choice (A) would delete the topic sentence from the paragraph. Choice (B) would put the second factor after the topic sentence that introduces it. Choice (D) is the concluding sentence and should not be eliminated. (Standards 10.5, 11.2)

120. (A)

Choice (A) eliminates the fragment in the second half of Part 4. The subject is "the use of speech," so the verb should be *facilitated* and not the infinitive *to facilitate*. Choice (B) would delete the necessary transition word *other*, needed to link developments discussed in the first paragraph with developments discussed in the second paragraph. Choice (C) changes the comparative degree *less*, needed to compare two items in Part 9, to the superlative degree needed to compare three or more things. Choice (D) changes the present participle *ensuring* to the past participle *ensured*. This change is incorrect because the present participle is necessary to show that survival is still going on; the past participle would indicate that survival has stopped. (Standards 7.1, 7.2)

MATHEMATICS

121. (C)

The useful, traditional approach to multiplying simple fractions (those between 0 and 1) is to first multiply the numerators together and then to multiply the denominators together to find the product. In this case, $\frac{3}{4} \times \frac{2}{3} = \frac{6}{12}$. That fraction is then shown in simplest form, $\frac{1}{2}$. (Standard 14.1)

122. (A)

The work can be set up like this:

$$0.05\overline{)6.2}$$

Dividing (while temporarily ignoring the zeros and decimal points) gives

$$
\begin{array}{r}
124 \\
0.05\overline{)6.2} \\
\underline{50} \\
12 \\
\underline{10} \\
20
\end{array}
$$

Next, you count the number of digits to the right of the decimal point in the divisor (two). Two, then, is the number of places that you shift the "inside" decimal point to the right, then "up" into the answer:

$$0.05 \overline{)6.2}^{\,124}$$

Because the answer is a whole number, the decimal point does not have to be shown. (Standard 14.1)

123. **(C)**

When subtraction involves any negative numbers, a good rule to use is, "Don't subtract the second number. Instead, add its opposite." Using that rule, the original expression, $(-36)-11$ becomes $(-36)+(-11)$. To be "in debt" by 36, then to be further "in debt" by 11, puts one "in debt" by 47, shown as -47. (Standard 14.1)

124. **(D)**

When presented with a simplification problem involving several different operations, the universally accepted order of operations must be used. In this case, working from left to right, the multiplication (6×2) and the division $(3 \div 3)$ must be completed first, giving $12 + 1$, or 13. (Standard 14.1)

125. **(A)**

One way to arrive at the answer is to set up an incomplete proportion, with one corner being

$$\frac{14}{x} = \frac{22}{100}$$

To complete the proportion (and to find the answer), you can cross-multiply 14 and 100, equaling 1400, which you then divide by 22, giving approximately 64.

Estimation works well for this problem too. Think of 22% as nearly 20%, or one-fifth. If 14 is one-fifth of something, you can multiply 14 by 5 to get you near the answer. $14 \times 5 = 70$, which is close to 64, or answer (A). (Standard 14.1)

126. **(C)**

Because multiplication is commutative (factors can be multiplied in any order), you multiply the 2 and the 6, giving 12; and 10^3 and 10^4, giving 10^7. (Note: To multiply exponential expressions with like bases, you add the exponents.) This gives 12×10^7.

That expression is not in scientific notation (the first number must be between 0 and 10), so you change the 12 into 1.2, and 10^7 into 10^8 to "compensate." (Standard 14.3)

127. **(A)**

Bob earned $6 an hour for three hours, or $18. Keyva babysat for six hours (twice as long as Bob), earning $7 each hour. That's $42. $18 + $42 = $60. (Standard 18.1)

128. **(C)**

To find the average (mean) of a set of values, first add them together. In this case, the negative and the positive integers should be added together separately. Those two sums are –12 and 5. (The zero can be ignored; it does not affect either sum.) Then –12 and 5 should be added together for a sum of –7.

To complete the work, the sum of –7 must be divided by the number of values (7), giving –1. (Standard 17.3)

129. **(D)**

The first price increase is for 10%. That's the same as one-tenth, and one-tenth of $40 is $4. Adding $4 to $40 gives $44 as the March price.

The next increase is 15% of $44. Multiplying 44 by 0.15 (0.15 being another way to represent 15%) gives 6.6, which is read as $6.60. You then increase the March price of $44 by $6.60, giving you $50.60.

Note that you cannot arrive at the answer by adding the individual percent increases (10 + 15 = 25) and then multiplying by 40. (Standard 14.1)

130. **(A)**

Finding the answer by setting up a proportion works well here:

$$\frac{3}{4.65} = \frac{5}{x}$$

Proportions often are two fractions set equal to each other, with one "corner" being the unknown value, or x. The equation above can be read as "3 is to 4.65 as 5 is to what?"

One way to solve a proportion (that is, to find the value of x), is to cross-multiply the two corners that have known values (in this case 4.65 and 5.) That gives 23.25, which is then divided by the remaining known value (3), giving 7.75. (Standard 14.2)

131. **(B)**

The percentage "0.2%" must be seen as "two-tenths of one percent" (and not as "two percent"). Given as a decimal numeral, 0.2% is 0.002. (You move the decimal point two places to the left when converting from a percent to a decimal numeral.)

You then multiply the starting population of 1620 by 0.002, giving 3.24, or approximately 3 people. Adding 3 to 1620 gives 1623. (Standard 14.4)

132. **(C)**

The chart shows that Madison received less than half of the votes (his slice takes up less than half of the pie), so statement I cannot be true.

Washington and Monroe together received 55% of the votes, and everyone else voted for Madison, so Madison must have received 45% of the votes (all of the candidates' percents must add up to 100%.) Statement II is therefore true.

Monroe received 30% of the 600 votes. 0.30 times 600 is 180, so statement III is true.

Madison received 45% of the vote, and 45% of 600 is 270, so statement IV is false. (Standard 17.1)

133. **(A)**

The somewhat steep straight line to the left tells you that Mr. Cain worked at a steady rate for awhile. The completely flat line in the middle tells you he stopped for a while—the line doesn't go up because no grass was cut then. Finally the line continues upward (after his break) less steeply (and therefore more flatly), indicating that he was working at a slower rate. (Standard 17.2)

134. **(B)**

Because Ms. Patton's increases were consistent ($3,000 annually), and because the directions tell you that only one statement is true, answer (B) must be correct. To be more confident however, you can examine the other statements:

The range of Ms. Patton's earnings is $12,000 (the jump from $30,000 to $42,000), not $15,000, so answer (A) cannot be correct.

Although Ms. Patton may have earned $45,000 in 2003, you don't know that, so answer (C) cannot be correct.

Answer (D) gives the incorrect earnings average; it was $36,000, not $38,000. (Standard 17.1)

135. **(D)**

It is helpful to make a sketch of the line on the coordinate plane. (To do to that you need to know how to plot individual points.)

The line "travels" from the lower left to the upper right, meaning that it has a positive slope. Statement II is therefore true. The y-intercept of a line is the spot at which the line crosses, or intercepts, the vertical axis. In this case, that's at point $(0, 4)$. (You can simply say that the y-intercept is 4, without mentioning the 0). Statement IV is therefore true as well. (Standard 16.1)

136. **(C)**

There are several methods for finding the slope of a line if two points are known. The most straightforward method is to use the slope formula:

$$m = \frac{y_2 - y_1}{x_2 - x_1}$$

This can be read as "the slope of a line (m) is equal to the difference of the y coordinates of any two points on the line ($y_2 - y_1$) divided by the difference of the x coordinates ($x_2 - x_1$).

For this problem, you subtract the first y coordinate from the second $[(-2) - 6]$, giving -8. You then do the same for the x coordinates $[4 - (-2)]$, giving 6. Dividing -8 by 6 is the same as showing the fraction $-\frac{8}{6}$ or, in lowest terms, $-\frac{4}{3}$. (Standard 16.1)

137. **(C)**

There are several ways to determine which equation matches the line. An easy way is to decide first whether the line has a positive or a negative slope. Because the line moves from the upper left to the lower right, you would say it has a negative slope.

In a linear equation of the form $y = mx + b$ (where y is isolated on the left side of the equation), the coefficient of x is the slope of the line. The y-intercept is represented by b, which in this case is 1. The only equation with a negative slope (-8) is response (C), so that is the correct answer.

Another clue that (C) is correct can be found by considering the apparent slope, or steepness of the line. The line in problem 17 is fairly steep, and a slope of -8 (or 8) is considered fairly steep too, suggesting that (C) is correct. (Standard 16.1)

138. **(D)**

The y-intercept of a linear equation is the point at which its graph passes through, or intercepts, the vertical y-axis. One way to determine the y-intercept is by rewriting the equation in y-intercept form:

$$y = mx + b$$

If a linear equation is in that form, b tells you where the graph of the line intercepts the y-axis. In this case, you rewrite (or transform) the equation following these steps:

$$2x = 3y - 12$$
$$3y - 12 = 2x$$
$$3y = 2x + 12$$
$$y = 2 \div 3x + 4$$

That final version of the equation is indeed in y-intercept form. The 4 tells you that the graph of the equation intercepts the y-axis at point $(0, 4)$. The answer cannot be (C) because $(-6, 0)$ is an x-intercept. (Standard 16.1)

139. **(A)**

Consider various random points in the shaded area: $(5, -2)$, $(-1, 2)$, $(12, 2.5)$ and $(-9, 1)$. Notice that all points in the shaded area have a y-coordinate value less than 3. The inequality that states this is the one in (A) ("y is less than 3.") (Standard 16.1)

140. **(C)**

Inverse variations give graphs that are curves. As equations, they take the forms $xy = k$ or $y = \dfrac{k}{x}$. The graph shown in problem 20 is simpler than that, so statement I is false.

The graphs of direct variations are straight lines that pass through the point $(0, 0)$ (the origin.) As equations, they take the form $y = mx + 0$, or simply $y = mx$. The line shown in problem 20 is the graph of a direct variation, so statement II is true.

Because point $(-5, 5)$ is equally distant from both the x- and y-axes, the line "cuts" quadrant II at a 45° angle. Lines that form 45° angles with the x- and y-axes (assuming the same scales on both axes) have slopes of 1 or -1. The line in problem 20 travels from upper left to lower right, meaning that its slope is negative, so statement III is also true. (Standard 16.1)

141. **(B)**

Just from looking at the graph, it's clear that most of the space under the curve is past the 60 mark on the *x*-axis. Answer (D) is eliminated because it doesn't include statement I.

Statement II can't be answered by what the graph shows. It appears possible that certain questions were too hard for many in the class and that there weren't enough questions to differentiate (B) students from (C) students, but perhaps the class performed exactly as it should have, given the students' ability and Ms. Alvarez's teaching. The distribution can give a teacher many clues about the test and the students and even herself, but by itself tells us nothing about the fairness of the test. Thus, answer (A) can be eliminated.

Statement III is also false; in left-skewed distributions such as this one, the median is higher than the mean. This is true because the mean is lowered by the lowest scores while the mean is relatively unaffected by them.

Statement IV is true: one fairly large group has scored in the high 80s and 90s and another discernible group in the low to mid-60s, whereas few students fall outside these two groups. Thus, the answer has to be (B). (Standard 17.3)

142. **(D)**

Using the rules for solving one-variable equations, the original equation is transformed as follows:

$$\frac{x}{3} - 9 = 15$$

Adding 9 to each side of the equation gives

$$\frac{x}{3} = 24$$

Multiplying both sides by 3 gives

$$x = 72 \text{ (Standard 16.2)}$$

143. **(A)**

Again, using the rules for solving one-variable equations produces these transformations:

$$3x^2 - 11 = 1$$

Adding 11 to each side of the equation gives

$$3x^2 = 12$$

Dividing both sides by 3 gives

$$x^2 = 4$$

You next find the square roots of 4; 2 and –2.

The solutions can be checked by substituting them (one at a time) into the original equation to see if they work. In this case, both 2 and –2 do indeed work. (Standard 16.2)

144. **(A)**

Solving for a particular variable in an equation means to isolate that variable on one side of the equation. In this case, use of the rules for transforming equations allows you to change the original equation into the desired one:

$$\frac{y}{3} - \frac{x}{2} = 4$$

Adding to each side gives

$$\frac{y}{3} = \frac{x}{2} + 4$$

Then, multiplying each side by 3 gives

$$y = \frac{3x}{2} + 12$$

(Standard 16.3)

145. **(D)**

One way to solve the problem is by writing a one-variable equation that matches the information given:

$$4x + 2(10 - x) = 26$$

The "$4x$" represents four tires for each car. You use x for the number of cars because at first, you don't know how many cars there are.

$(10 - x)$ represents the number of motorcycle tires in the lot. (If there are ten vehicles total, and x of them are cars, you subtract x from 10 to get the number of "leftover" motorcycles.) Then $2(10 - x)$ stands for the number of motorcycle tires in the lot.

You know that the sum of the values $4x$ and $2(10 - x)$ is 26, and that gives you your equation. Using the standard rules for solving a one-variable equation, you find that x (the number of cars in the lot) equals 3.

Another approach to the problem when given multiple answer choices is to try substituting each answer for the unknown variable in the problem to see which one makes sense. (Standard 18.2)

146. **(A)**

You know that the correct equation must show three consecutive odd numbers being added to give 117. Odd numbers (just like even numbers) are two apart from each other. Only the three values given in answer (A) are each two apart.

Because the numbers being sought are odd, one might be tempted to choose answer (D). However, the second value in answer (D) $(x + 1)$ is not two numbers apart from the first value (x); it's different by only one. (Standard 18.2)

147. **(D)**

All riders must pay at least three dollars, so 3 will be added to the cost of the fare. Only answers (B) and (D) meet that requirement. The additional fare of two dollars "for every mile or fraction of a mile" tells you that you will need to multiply the number of miles driven (you use 11 because of the extra fraction of a mile) by 2, leading you to answer (D). (Standard 18.2)

148. **(C)**

Belinda used a specific observation (that all the birds she saw could fly) and inferred a general statement (all birds can fly). This is an example of inductive reasoning so statement III is correct. However, not all inductive reasoning statements are necessarily true. In this case, Belinda is not correct as there are numerous birds that cannot fly. (Standards 15.1, 15.3)

149. **(C)**

On each consecutive day, Juan is doubling the amount of pennies he is placing in his piggy bank. If he continues doubling . . . 8, 16, 32, 64, 128, 256, . . . , he would end up placing 512 pennies in his piggy bank on day 10. (Sandard 15.2)

150. **(A)**

In your sample you have a ratio of $\dfrac{7}{25}$. This is from the fact that you have 7 yellow gumballs out of 25 in your handful. You would set this ratio equal to $\dfrac{x}{1000}$ (the ratio of total yellow gumballs to the total gumballs) and solve the proportion $\dfrac{7}{25} = \dfrac{x}{1000}$. The answer to this proportion is 280 yellow gumballs. (Standard 14.2)

151. **(D)**

Since the profits are rising as the months go by, a positive correlation exists. Estimating July's profits means that it should be up from June's profit, so the profit should be $33,000, not $25,000. Therefore, II and IV are true statements and the answer is (D). (Standards 17.4, 18.4)

152. **(A)**

In looking at the chart in Chapter 5, you can see that there are 7 different ways you can get a sum that is a multiple of 5. There are 4 ways to roll a sum of 5, and 3 ways to roll of sum of 10. There are a total of 36 different sums, so the probability of rolling a sum that is a multiple of 5 is $\frac{7}{36}$. (Standards 17.5)

153. **(C)**

In looking at the following tree diagram, you can see that the probability of drawing a green crayon and flipping a heads is $\frac{3}{16}$.

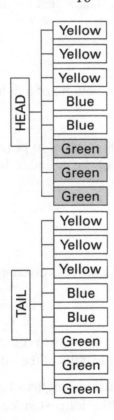

(Standard 17.5)

154. **(A)**

Given that there are a total of 25 students and 3 (the number in the overlap of dogs and cats) of them have a dog and a cat, the probability is $\frac{3}{25}$. (Standard 17.5)

155. **(D)**

Since the mean is higher than the median, this is a right-skewed distribution. (Standard 17.4)

156. **(B)**

Angle *xyz* is an inscribed angle (its vertex is on the circle). Angle *xcz* is a central angle (its vertex is at the circle's center). When two such angles intercept (or "cut off") the same arc of the circle, there exists a specific size relationship between the two angles. The measure of the central angle will always be double the measure of the inscribed angle. In this case, that means that the measure of angle *xcz* must be 80°.

That means that minor arc *xz* also has measure 80°. Every circle (considered as an arc) has measure 360°. That means that major arc *xyz* has measure 280° (360° − 80°). (Standard 16.4)

157. **(A)**

The formula for finding the volume of a cylinder is:

$$V = \pi r^2 h$$

This means that the volume is equal to pi (about 3.14) times the measure of the radius squared times the height of the cylinder. In this case, that's

$3.14 \times 6^2 \times 8$

or

$3.14 \times 36 \times 8$

or about 904. (Note that the final answer is given in cubic centimeters.) (Standard 16.5)

158. **(B)**

You can use the Pythagorean theorem to compute the length of any side of any right triangle, as long as you know the lengths of the other two sides. Here is the theorem:

For any right triangle with side lengths of *a*, *b*, and *c*, and where *a* is the length of the hypotenuse (the longest side, and the one opposite the right angle), $a^2 = b^2 + c^2$.

Substituting the real values for a and b from problem 38, you get

$a^2 = 11^2 + 5^2$

or

$a^2 = 146$

To complete the work, you take the (positive) square root of 146, which is slightly over 12 ($12 \times 12 = 144$). (Standard 18.3)

159. **(A)**

To find the total square feet of the wall you would multiply 8 feet by 12 feet and get 96 square feet. However, you need to subtract the area of the window. So, you would multiply 3 feet by 5 feet, to arrive at 15 square feet. Subtracting the 15 square feet from the 96 square feet, you have a total of 81 square feet to paint. The paint is $1.50 per square yard. Therefore, you need to convert the square feet to square yards. One square yard is 9 square feet, so you would divide the 81 square feet by 9. When you get the answer of 9, this is 9 square yards. You would then multiply the 9 square yards by $1.50 to a total of $13.50 to paint the wall. (Standard 18.3)

160. **(C)**

When two parallel lines are crossed by another line (called a transversal), eight angles are formed. There are, however, only two angle measures among the eight angles, and the sum of the two measures will be 180°. All of the smaller angles will have the same measures, and all of the larger angles will have the same measures. In this case, the smaller angles all measure 50°, so the larger angles (including angle y) all measure 130°. (Standard 16.4)

161. **(A)**

There are two things one must know in order to answer the question. One is the meaning of the small square at the vertex of angle *BXC*. That symbol tell you that angle *BXC* is a right angle (one with 90°.) You must also understand that a straight line can be thought of as an angle that measures 180°. This is a straight angle.

Therefore, the sum of the angles (D) *XC* (42°) and *BXC* (90°) is 132°. This means that the remaining angle on the line must have measure 48° (180° − 132°). (Standard 16.4)

162. **(A)**

If you know the measures of two angles of any triangle, you can compute the measure of the third angle. (The sum of the three angles is always 180°.) So the measure of the third angle in both of the triangles is 50°, and statement III is correct.

If two triangles have the same degree measures (as established above), then they are similar triangles. (This means that they have the same shape.) Statement I is therefore correct.

Triangles are congruent only if they are exactly the same shape and size. One triangle is larger than the other, so statement II is false.

Because the second triangle is larger than the first, and they're the same shape, there is no way that sides BC and YZ could be the same length. Statement IV is thus false. (Standard 16.5)

163. **(D)**

This is a problem of deduction. That is, the answer can be deduced from the information given. One solution to this problem is to make a list of the boys' names based on what you know. You could start by taking the very first bit of information, "Fred beat Matt." This allows you to stack those two names

Fred
Matt

with Fred at the top because he was the faster of the two boys.

Then, instead of just taking the next piece of information ("Curt beat Dwayne"), you could instead look for information that tells you more about the boys already listed. You read, for instance, that Dwayne beat Fred. This allows you to add Dwayne to the list:

Dwayne
Fred
Matt

By filling in the other boys' names based on the information given, you should produce the following list:

Pat
Curt
Dwayne
Fred
Matt
Ivan

This shows that Ivan was last in the race. (Standard 15.2)

164. **(C)**

    To solve this problem, you need to first change each mixed number into an improper fraction. Eight and one-third becomes 25-thirds and one and two-thirds becomes five-thirds. Then perform the following computation:

$$\frac{25}{3} \div \frac{5}{3} \text{ which becomes}$$

$$\frac{25}{3} \times \frac{3}{5} = \frac{5}{1} \times \frac{1}{1}$$

    which equals 5 (Standard 14.1)

165. **(B)**

    Since the data is organized by color, it is considered categorical data. Categorical data is discrete not continuous and cannot be considered skewed or normally distributed. (Standard 17.2)

166. **(D)**

    Since there are 3 icons that represent 12 candies in the "green" row, you can conclude that each icon represents 4 candies. Since there are 9 icons in the "red" row, you multiply 9 by 4 and conclude that there are 36 "red" candies. (Standard 17.1)

167. **(B)**

    The label would be the surface area of the side of the jar. The side of the jar is a rectangular shape with a length that is the circumference of the jar $[(C) = 2\pi r]$. Therefore, you take 2π times the radius and arrive at 6π cm. When you multiply this by the height of 15 cm, you arrive at 90π square centimeters. (Standards 16.5, 18.3)

168. **(B)**

    This situation is an exponential situation, with the mold doubling on each consecutive day. Since the first doubling actually occurs on day two, the exponent on "2" needs to be reduced by 1. This doubling needs to be multiplied by the original area of mold, 6 square inches. Therefore, answer (B) is the equation you would use to determine the amount of mold on the "nth" day. (Standard 18.2)

169. **(D)**

    Twenty-three and three-fourths inches is approximately 24 inches which is approximately 2 feet. When you multiply 5 times 2 (5 shelves times 2 feet), you would need approximately 10 linear feet of shelving. (Standards 14.3, 14.4)

170. **(C)**

To solve in terms of "*y*" you would follow these steps:

$$2x - 3y = 6$$

$$2x - 2x - 3y = 6 - 2x$$

$$-3y = 6 - 2x$$

$$1y = -2 + \frac{2}{3}x$$

$$y = \frac{2}{3}x - 2$$

$$y = \frac{2}{3}x - 2 \text{ (Standard 16.3)}$$

WRITING EXAMPLES

Writing Sample with a High Range Score of 6 or 5

		Focus	Support/ Elaboration	Organization	Grammar and Conventions
SCORE	6 or 5	The writing sample that receives a high range score exhibits an introduction, thesis, and conclusion that are clearly aligned.	The writing sample that receives a high range score exhibits strong, consistent, and fully supported elaborative and varied ideas.	The writing sample that receives a high range score exhibits an effective and clear vertical plan, logical structure, and horizontal connections. It also uses effective transitions to signal vertical and horizontal relationships.	The writing sample that receives a high range score exhibits very few errors. The sentence structure is effective and varied. Usage of grammar and conventions is precise throughout.

The Literature of the Past

The direction of modern literary scholarship points toward an alarming conclusion. The depreciation of the literary study of bygone periods is a sign of two disturbing trends. First, scholars are avoiding more difficult study in preference to what seems light or facile. Furthermore, the neglect of the literature of former eras is a denial of the contribution that past authors have made toward modern literature. This is not to suggest that all scholars who study modern literature do so because they are either intimidated by past literature or do not appreciate its value. However, the shrinking minority of past literary scholarship is a clear indication that intimidation and awe of past conventions are deterrents to many students of literature.

The dread associated with past literature reflects poorly upon our society. The attempts to simplify literature to accommodate simpler audiences has resulted in a form of literary deflation. The less society taxes its audience's minds, the less comprehensive those unexercised minds become. Information and ideas are now transmitted to the average man through the shallow medium of television programming. Modern students are evolving from this medium, and the gap separating them from the complexity of the classics is continuing to grow.

Once more, it is important to stress that this essay does not seek to diminish students of modern literature. The only demand this argument makes upon modern students is that they supplement their study with significant portions of the classics from which all subsequent literature has been derived, whether consciously or unconsciously. Failure to do so is an act akin to denying the importance of history itself. Like history, literature exists as an evolutionary process; modern literature can only have come into existence through the development of past literature.

Concerning the relative complexity of the classics to modern literature, the gap is not so great as one may think. Surely, one who glances at the works of Shakespeare or Milton without prior exposure will be daunted by them. However, a disciplined mind can overcome the comprehensive barriers erected over the past few centuries through persistence and perseverance.

Unfortunately, the ability to overcome the barriers to past literature may eventually become obsolete. The more frequently students select their courses of study through fear rather than interest, the wider the literary gap will become, until the pampered minds of all future readers will prove unequal to the task of reading the literature of our fathers. The more frequently students deny the usefulness of the literature antedating this century, the more frequently they deny their own literary heritage, the more probable it will become for modern literature's structure to crumble through lack of a firm foundation.

Features of the Writing Sample Scoring 6 or 5

Focus

The essay follows the course presented in the topic paragraph, reemphasizing major points such as the writer's reluctance to condemn all modern scholars. This emphasis is not straight repetition, but carries different viewpoints and evidence for the writer's argument. The digression on television in the second paragraph neatly rounds off the writer's overall concern for cultural consequences of historical literature's depreciation.

Support/Elaboration

The paper's topic and the writer's viewpoint are both well laid out in the first paragraph. The two trends described by the author in the topic paragraph are explored in deeper detail throughout the essay. The language and style fit the writer's audience. The style is formal, but possesses a personalized voice.

The writer follows the suggestions of the writing assignment closely, structuring his essay around the reflections and discussions listed therein. Each paragraph bears an example to lend authority to the writer's argument.

The second paragraph uses the theory of television's vegetative influence. The third paragraph utilizes the evolutionary equality of history. The fourth paragraph evokes names that the reader can relate to in terms of comprehensive difficulty.

Organization

Many transitional conventions are utilized. "Once more . . ."; "Concerning the relative complexity . . ."; "Unfortunately . . ." The examples throughout the paragraphs have a pointed direction. The concluding paragraph completes the argument with a premonition of future calamity should its warning go unheeded.

Grammar and Conventions

The sentences are standardized and vary in form, although some passive constructions ("will be daunted," "the more probable it will become") might have been avoided. The repetition of "the more frequently" in the final paragraph is particularly effective and pointed.

Words are chosen to offer variety. "Past literature" is supplemented by "literary study of bygone days" and "the literature of former eras." Phrasing is consistent and standard, although the third sentence of the second paragraph ("The less society taxes . . . the less comprehensive") is slightly awkward, though the repetition does achieve some effect.

Spelling and punctuation are mostly standard throughout the essay. The sentences in the final paragraph might be divided and shortened, although this may diminish their effect.

Writing Sample With a Mid-Range Score of 4 or 3

	Focus	Support/ Elaboration	Organization	Grammar and Conventions
SCORE 4 or 3	The writing sample that receives a mid-range score has a purpose that is either inferred or adequately stated. The thesis in general may be appropriate and logical or may drift in focus. The conclusion may be non-existent, repetitive, or just a restatement of the thesis.	The writing sample that receives a mid-range score has major points that are partially to adequately supported. Elaboration may be uneven or lack depth.	The writing sample that receives a mid-range score exhibits a coherence that is partially to generally maintained by a vertical plan. Cohesion is partially to generally maintained by horizontal sequencing. Transitions may or may not be used to signal horizontal and vertical connections.	The writing sample that receives a mid-range score exhibits minor and a few major errors; however they do not interfere with construction of meaning. The sentence structure is adequate. Usage of grammar and conventions is adequate, although at times imprecise.

Modern Literature

It doesn't matter whether or not we read past literature. Past literature has been converted into what we now know as "modern literature". The elements of the past are therefore incorporated into the body of what we now have.

When we read a work of modern literature based upon the classics, such as Joyce's *Ulysses*, it doesn't matter whether or not we've read Homer's *Odyssey*. What matters is what Joyce made out of Homer's epic; not what Homer started out with.

When we see *West Side Story* in the movies, it doesn't matter whether or not we've read *Romeo and Juliet*: the end result is the same; therefore, we do not need to know the original source. I don't think it makes a difference whether or not we even recognize Tony and Maria as Romeo and Juliet. Tony and Maria are today's versions of Romeo and Juliet, and they match the culture that they are told in.

It has been said that all of the good plots have been used up by past ages, and that all we create now are variations of those plots. This statement is false. It is rather the case that these plots are universal variables that each age must interpret in its own unique way. I find it rather faseatious to study the interpretation of other cultures. We should be concerned only with our own.

Past literature is not necessary in a modern world that has reformed the mistakes of the past. Anything that hasn't carried over from the past is negligible: what was good for Shakespeare's audience may not be what we need. In conclusion, I would have to strongly conclude that the "trend of studying modern versus past literature" is commendable, and not contemptible.

Features of the Writing Sample Scoring 4 or 3

Focus

Though the writer knows the point he is trying to promote, his evidence is presented haphazardly and without a logical design. However, his rather abrupt conclusion is somewhat supported by his points.

Support/Elaboration

The main topic is not supplied directly within the work. Though the reader is aware of the conflict between modern and past literature, there is no sense of scholarly consensus as suggested by the writing assignment. The writer's somewhat informal style is unbalanced throughout the work by his uncertainty with his audience.

The essay does not follow a logical pattern; one premise does not meld fluidly into another. Though the premises loosely support the conclusion, they do not support each other.

Organization

Transitions are slight, if any. The repetition of "when we" in the opening two paragraphs is noticeable. Each point should have been further developed. The writer assumes his reader is quite familiar with *West Side Story* and its characters.

Grammar and Conventions

Most sentences follow standard sentence structure, although some are very irregular. The first sentence of paragraph three expresses two or three independent thoughts and should be separated accordingly. The final sentence of the fourth paragraph contains an unclear modifier: "own" should read either "own interpretation" or "own culture."

Most words are used in their proper context, and an attempt has been made to use some erudite words. "End result" is redundant; "end" should have been excluded. The declaration "this statement is false" in the fourth paragraph is not supported by logical evidence. In this case, the writer should have asserted that this was his own opinion. However, in other cases it is recommended that the writer be bold with assertions. A degree of proof is all that is required to make those assertions. "In conclusion" is redundant with "conclude" in the final sentence of the essay. Contractions such as "we've" and "don't" should be written out in their long forms.

Most words are spelled properly, although "faseatious" should be spelled "facetious." (The period in the second sentence of the first paragraph should lie within the quotation marks.) The comma after "commendable" in the final paragraph should be eliminated because it does not introduce a new clause.

Writing Sample with a Low-Range Score of 2

	Focus	Support/ Elaboration	Organization	Grammar and Conventions
SCORE 6 or 5	The writing sample that receives a low-range score has a purpose that is vague or prompt-dependent. The thesis in general may be inappropriate to the topic and contain unrelated illogical or redundant ideas. The conclusion, if present, may be unrelated.	The writing sample that receives a low-range score has few points, if any, with support and elaboration given.	The writing sample that receives a low-range score exhibits little evidence of vertical or horizontal plan. Transitions, if present, are disjointed.	The writing sample that receives a low-range score exhibits many minor and major errors which interfere with construction of meaning. The sentence structure maybe fragmentary or rambling. Usage of grammar and conventions is imprecise.

Literature

Modern literature is no better than past literature, and vice-versa. It is interest that matters. If people aren't interested in the past, then so be it. A famous man once said "To each his own". I agree.

For example, you can see that books are getting easier and easier to understand. This is a good thing, because more knowledge may be comunicated this way. Comunication is what literature is all about: Some people comunicate with the past, and others with the present.

I communicate with the present. I'm not saying we all should. It's all up to your point of view. When a scholer chooses past over present, or vice-versa, that's his perogative. It doesn't make him better or worse than anybody else. We should all learn to accept each other's point of view.

When I read someone like Fitzgerald or Tolkien, I get a different feeling than Shakespeare. Shakespeare can inspire many people, but I just don't get that certain feeling from his plays. "The Hobbit," "The Great Gatsby," "Catcher in the Rye," and "Of Mice and Men." These are all great classics from this century. We should be proud of them. However, some people prefer "The Trojan War" and "Beowulf." Let them have it. Remember: 'To each his own."

Features of the Writing Sample Scoring 2

Focus

The writer seems to contradict her own points at times, favoring modern literature rather than treating the subject as objectively as she had proposed. It is clear that the writer's train of thought shifted during the essay. This was covered up by ending with the catch phrase, "to each his own."

Support/Elaboration

The writer attempts to angle her argument in different ways by presenting such concepts as "communication" and "point of view." However, her thought processes are abrupt and underdeveloped.

The writer misconstrues the topic and writes about the relative worth of modern and past literature. The topic does not call for a judgment of period literatures; it calls for a perspective on the way in which they are studied. Her personal style is too familiar; it is unclear to whom the essay is addressed.

Organization

There is neither direction nor logical flow in the essay. One point follows the next without any transition or connection. All three persons are used to prove her argument: the writer resorts to "I," "you," and "a famous man." There is no clear overall thesis guiding the essay.

Grammar and Conventions

Some sentences follow standard formation. Sentence three of the final paragraph is a fragment. The sentences are short and choppy, as is the thought they convey. Too many sentences are merely brief remarks on the preceding statements (e.g., "I agree," "Let them have it," etc.). These are not appropriate because they do not evoke new thought. The reference to Shakespeare in the first sentence of the final paragraph implies more than the writer intended. It should read: "than when I read Shakespeare."

Many words are repeated without any attempt to supply synonyms (e.g., "communication," "past"). Colloquial expressions are widespread and should be avoided. *The Trojan War* is evidently an improper reference to Homer's *Iliad*.

There are many mechanical errors. Punctuation and spelling are inconsistent. "Comunication" and "comunicate" are spelled improperly in paragraph two, while "communicate" is spelled correctly in paragraph three. "Scholer" should be spelled "scholar." "Perogative" should be spelled "prerogative." In the fourth sentence of the first paragraph, the period should lie within the quotation marks, as it does in the final sentence of the essay. The book titles in sentences three and six of the final paragraph should be underlined with no quotation marks.

Writing Sample with a Score of 1, U, or B

An essay with a score of 1 demonstrates few writing elements and most elements are non-existent or are incorrectly used.

A response given a U is deemed unscorable. A U score would be given if the essay is not on the given topic, is illegible, too short, or not written in English.

A response given a B means that the writer submitted a blank sheet that contained no answer.

Appendix

The skills addressed in this subarea require demonstration of literal, inferential, and critical reading skills in a variety of written materials—including college-level texts and original source documents—in the areas of physical and life sciences, humanities and fine arts, and the social and behavioral sciences.

Standard 1   Determine the meaning of words and phrases in context.

The following are examples of content that may be covered under this standard.

1.1   Use context clues to determine the meaning of unfamiliar words or words with multiple meanings.

1.2   Recognize the correct use of commonly misused pairs (e.g., affect/effect) in a passage.

1.3   Determine the meaning of figurative or colloquial language in a passage.

1.4   Identify appropriate synonyms or antonyms for words in a passage.

Standard 2   **Understand the main idea and supporting details in written material.**

The following are examples of content that may be covered under this standard.

2.1   Identify the stated main idea of a paragraph or passage.

2.2   Establish the sequence of events or steps presented in a passage.

2.3   Recognize information that supports, illustrates, or elaborates the main idea of a paragraph or a passage.

2.4   Identify the meaning of a figurative expression in a passage.

Standard 3   **Apply skills of inference and interpretation to a variety of written materials.**

The following are examples of content that may be covered under this standard.

3.1   Recognize a writer's implied purpose for writing (e.g., to persuade, to describe).

3.2   Identify the statement that best expresses the implied main idea of a paragraph or passage.

3.3   Recognize implied cause-and-effect relationships in a passage.

3.4   Interpret the content, word choice, and phrasing of a passage to determine a writer's opinions, point of view, or position on an issue.

Standard 4   **Analyze relationships among ideas in written material.**

The following are examples of content that may be covered under this standard.

4.1   Recognize similarities and differences among ideas in a passage.

4.2   Analyze relationships between ideas in opposition (e.g., pro and con).

4.3   Select solutions to problems based on information presented in written material.

4.4   Draw conclusions from information stated or implied in a passage.

Standard 5 **Use critical reasoning skills to evaluate written material.**

The following are examples of content that may be covered under this standard.

5.1 Recognize stated or implied assumptions on which the validity of an argument depends.

5.2 Determine the relevance of specific facts, examples, or graphic data to a writer's argument.

5.3 Recognize fallacies in the logic of a writer's argument.

5.4 Recognize qualifying language and distinguish between fact and opinion in written material.

5.5 Assess the credibility, objectivity, or bias of the author of a passage or the author's sources.

Standard 6 **Apply skills for outlining and summarizing written materials and interpreting information presented in graphs or tables.**

The following are examples of content that may be covered under this standard.

6.1 Organize the main ideas in a passage into an outline or another form of graphic or tabular organization.

6.2 Identify an accurate summary of a passage.

6.3 Interpret information presented in charts, graphs, or tables.

SUBAREA II—LANGUAGE ARTS

The skills addressed in this subarea require demonstration of the ability to write effectively at the college level, with control over the conventions of edited English in the United States and competence in drafting, organizing, and revising written work, as well as the ability to exercise critical thinking and reflection in written communications.

A. Grammar and Usage

Standard 7   **Demonstrate command of standard usage in edited English in the United States.**

The following are examples of content that may be covered under this standard.

7.1   Understand the standard use of verbs (e.g., subject-verb agreement, verb tense, consistency of tense).

7.2   Identify and apply the standard use of pronouns (e.g., pronoun-antecedent agreement, standard pronoun case, use of possessive pronouns, standard use of relative and demonstrative pronouns).

7.3   Recognize and apply the standard use of modifiers (e.g., adverbs, adjectives, prepositional phrases).

Standard 8   **Understand and apply knowledge of mechanical conventions in edited English in the United States.**

The following are examples of content that may be covered under this standard.

8.1   Recognize instances in which incorrect or extraneous punctuation has been used or necessary punctuation has been omitted.

8.2   Identify standard initial capitalization and standard capitalization with proper words and titles.

8.3   Recognize the standard spelling of words.

B. Writing

Standard 9 **Understand the role of purpose and audience in written communication.**

The following are examples of content that may be covered under this standard.

9.1 Assess the appropriateness of written material for a specific purpose or audience (e.g., a business letter, a communication to parents).

9.2 Determine the likely effect on an audience of a writer's choice of a particular word or words (e.g., to evoke sympathy, to raise questions about an opposing point of view).

9.3 Identify persuasive techniques used by a writer in a passage.

9.4 Demonstrate the ability to adapt forms, organizational strategies, and styles for different audiences and purposes.

Standard 10 **Understand unity, focus, development, and organization in writing.**

The following are examples of content that may be covered under this standard.

10.1 Identify organizational methods used by the author of a passage.

10.2 Distinguish between effective and ineffective thesis statements.

10.3 Recognize unnecessary shifts in point of view (e.g., shifts from first to third person) or distracting details that impair development of the main idea in a passage.

10.4 Select appropriate and effective supporting material.

10.5 Recognize examples of focused, concise, and well-developed writing.

Standard 11 **Understand and apply editing and revision strategies.**

The following are examples of content that may be covered under this standard.

11.1 Apply editing and revision strategies affecting diction, syntax, transitions, organization, clarity, coherence, and point of view.

11.2 Make revisions that improve the unity and focus of a passage or that improve cohesion and the effective sequence of ideas.

11.3   Improve the clarity and effectiveness of a passage through changes in word choice.

11.4   Eliminate or replace unnecessary or imprecise words and phrases.

11.5   Insert appropriate transitional words or phrases (e.g., *however, as a result*) in a passage to convey the structure of the text and to help readers understand the sequence of a writer's ideas.

Standard 12   Recognize sentences and paragraphs that effectively communicate intended messages.

The following are examples of content that may be covered under this standard.

12.1   Demonstrate an understanding of unity within paragraphs and apply methods for enhancing paragraph organization and unity.

12.2   Recognize effective topic sentences and distinguish between effective and ineffective development of ideas within a paragraph.

12.3   Identify sentence fragments and run-on sentences.

12.4   Recognize wordiness, redundancy, and ineffective repetition in sentences and paragraphs.

12.5   Recognize inefficiency in sentence and paragraph construction.

C.   WRITING ASSIGNMENT

Standard 13   Prepare an organized, developed composition in edited English as used in the United States in response to instructions regarding content, purpose, and audience.

The following are examples of content that may be covered under this standard.

13.1   Compose a unified, focused, and sustained piece of writing on a given topic using language and style appropriate to a specified audience, purpose, and occasion.

13.2   Take a position on a contemporary social or political issue and defend that position with reasoned arguments and supporting examples.

13.3 Use effective sentence structure and apply the standards of edited English in the United States.

13.4 Demonstrate the ability to spell, capitalize, and punctuate according to the standards of edited English in the United States.

SUBAREA III—MATHEMATICS

The skills addressed in this subarea require demonstration of quantitative literacy at the college level through the application of mathematical methods and reasoning to the solution of real-world problems.

Standard 14 **Solve problems involving integers, fractions, decimals, and units of measurement.**

The following are examples of content that may be covered under this standard.

14.1 Solve problems involving integers, fractions, and decimals, including percentages.

14.2 Solve problems involving ratios and proportions.

14.3 Solve problems involving units of measurement, including U.S. customary and metric measurements, and conversions, including scientific notation (e.g., 6.05×10^8).

14.4 Use estimation skills to solve problems.

Standard 15 **Apply mathematical reasoning skills to analyze patterns and solve problems.**

The following are examples of content that may be covered under this standard.

15.1 Draw conclusions using inductive reasoning.

15.2 Draw conclusions using deductive reasoning.

15.3 Identify errors in mathematical explanations.

Standard 16   Solve problems involving algebra and geometry.

The following are examples of content that may be covered under this standard.

16.1   Graph numbers or number relationships.

16.2   Find the value of the unknown in a given one-variable equation.

16.3   Express one variable in terms of a second variable in two-variable equations.

16.4   Solve problems involving lines and angles.

16.5   Solve problems involving two- and three-dimensional geometric figures (e.g., perimeter and area problems, volume and surface area problems).

Standard 17   Understand concepts and procedures related to data analysis and statistics.

The following are examples of content that may be covered under this standard.

17.1   Interpret information from tables, line graphs, bar graphs, histograms, pictographs, and pie charts.

17.2   Recognize appropriate representations of various data in graphic form (discrete and continuous).

17.3   Demonstrate an understanding of fundamental statistical concepts (e.g., mean, correlation, standard deviation).

17.4   Interpret graphic and nongraphic representations of frequency distributions, percentiles, central tendency, variability, and correlation.

17.5   Demonstrate knowledge of basic concepts of probability using a variety of representations (e.g., word problems, Venn diagrams, tree diagrams).

Standard 18 **Solve applied problems using a combination of mathematical skills (including word problems involving one and two variables).**

The following are examples of content that may be covered under this standard.

18.1   Apply combinations of mathematical skills to solve a series of related problems.

18.2   Identify an equation to solve word problems involving one and two variables.

18.3   Apply number concepts and geometric principles to solve practical problems.

18.4   Apply statistical principles to analyze patterns and trends in data.

Index

NOTES

NOTES

NOTES

NOTES

NOTES

NOTES